American Film Institute

DATE DUE

OC 21 '03		
NO 9 FV		
OC 4 08		
NO 8 '05		
DE 16 06		
JE 19 08		
MY 20 10		
SE 21 10		
NO 3 '09		

DEMCO 38-296

DONA C

D1052591

Riverside Community College
Library
4800 Magnolia Avenue
Riverside, CA 92506

Macmillan • USA

SEP '01

PN1996 .C813 1997
Cooper, Dona.
Writing great screenplays
for film and TV

Second Edition

Macmillan General Reference
1633 Broadway
New York, NY 10019

Copyright © 1997, 1994 by Dona Cooper
All rights reserved
including the right of reproduction
in whole or in part in any form

An Arco Book

ARCO is a registered trademark of Simon & Schuster, Inc.
MACMILLAN is a registered trademark of Macmillan, Inc.

Library of Congress Card Catalog Number: 97-070076
ISBN: 0-02-861555-7

Manufactured in the United States of America

    4 5 6 7 8 9 10

Book Design: A&D Howell Design
Cover Design: Nick Anderson

Dedication

*To Oliver Hailey, who helped me appreciate
both the art and craft of writing.*

Acknowledgments

I would like to express deep thanks to:

Jan Wildman, for her creative insights, clear thinking, and dedication to the cause

Barbara Gilson, for her patience and wisdom

Sarah Ban Breathnach and Marcia Bartusiak, for sharing their war stories

Colette Wilson and Jan Cerveny, for their help and humor

And always, my husband, Arthur Popov, and my sister, Connie Cooper, for their constant love and support

Contents

The American Film Institute

The American Film Institute (AFI) is America's national arts organization dedicated to advancing and preserving the art of film, television, and other forms of the moving image. AFI's programs promote innovation and excellence through teaching, presenting, preserving, and redefining this art form.

From its campus in Los Angeles, located in the hills above Hollywood, AFI has for thirty years served as a point of national focus and coordination for the many individuals and institutions which make up the moving image community. In this effort, AFI is guided by four primary goals:

- training the next generation of American filmmakers
- presenting the moving image in its many forms to a national and international public
- preserving our nation's moving image heritage
- redefining the moving image

Since the AFI was founded in 1967, its original mandate—to bring together leading artists and educators who support film and television as an art form — has expanded to include all aspects of the moving image. With many new successes, such as the AFI Showcase at Walt Disney World in Florida, AFI's recent discovery of the oldest surviving American feature film, and the AFI Web site's presentation of complete classic Hollywood movies on the World Wide Web, the institute's influence continues to grow. Today, AFI is also playing a major role within the entertainment community to understand the new digital era and how this new media will impact the future of storytelling.

AFI has also moved beyond its status as a traditional not-for-profit organization. The institute has become a model not-for-profit for the 21st century through an entrepreneurial approach to the marketing and merchandising of AFI projects, programs, and other acitivities.

Guided by a distinguished board of trustees that includes prominent members of the creative community, business and academia, and led by the strong and stable leadership of Director and CEO Jean Picker Firstenberg and Co-Director and COO James Hindman, AFI looks to the future as one of America's leading national arts organizations.

American Film Institute Staff

Jean Picker Firstenberg
Director and CEO

James Hindman
Co-Director and COO
Provost, Center for Advanced Film
and Television Studies

Bruce Neiner
Associate Director
Finance and Administration

Victoria Silverman
Director
Development

Ken Wlaschin
Director
Creative Affairs

Frank Pierson
Director
Center for Advanced Film and
Television Studies

Debra Henderson
Director
Education and Training

Greg Lukow
Director, Administration
National Center for Film and
Video Preservation

Seth Oster
Director
Communications

History of the American Film Institute

In 1965, President Lyndon B. Johnson signed legislation creating the National Endowment for the Arts (NEA), saying:

> *We will create an American Film Institute that will bring together leading artists of the film industry, outstanding educators, and young men and women who wish to pursue this 20th century art form as their life's work.*

In turn, the NEA funded a report by the Stanford Research Institute that defined the need for and functions of the new American Film Institute. This report led to the founding of the institute in 1967. AFI was established with initial funding from the NEA, the Motion Picture Association of America and the Ford Foundation.

Gregory Peck served as the first chairman of AFI's original 22-member Board of Trustees, which included Sidney Poitier (vice chair), Francis Ford Coppola, Arthur Schlesinger, Jr., and Jack Valenti, president of the Motion Picture Association of America.

George Stevens, Jr. was named AFI's first director on June 5, 1965. His leadership characterized the first 12 years of AFI's evolution and growth. Succeeding Stevens in 1980 was Jean Picker Firstenberg, who continues to serve as AFI director and CEO. In 1996, Tom Pollock, former vice chairman of MCA, was elected to serve as the chairman of AFI's Board of Trustees.

In September 1989, President George Bush hosted AFI's 25th anniversary celebration in Washington, D.C. "Back to the Rose Garden" was a commemoration of President Johnson's signing of the legislation which led to AFI's establishment. The gala event was attended by hundreds of prominent Americans, including members of Congress, the diplomatic corps, business and academia, and, of course, the entertainment and creative community, led by distinguished filmmakers including Steven Spielberg, George Lucas, Martin Scorsese and Charlton Heston. At the time, President Bush said:

For almost a quarter century, the American Film Institute has nurtured and celebrated the art of the moving image. In doing so, it has had an immense impact on the mind and soul of America.

AFI identifies and trains America's next generation of moving image artists through the prestigious AFI Conservatory, the Directing Workshop for Women, and the Television Writer's Workshop. The education and training programs are dedicated to the vision of the artist as storyteller, providing an environment renowned for creativity and practical hands-on training. Some of the most successful filmmakers have graduated from AFI, including Bob Mandell, Michael Dinner, David Lynch, John McTiernan, Jon Avnet, Marshall Herskovitz, Ed Zwick, Carl Franklin, and Amy Heckerling. In 1985, the Conservatory became the first film school to be accredited by the National Association of Schools of Art and Design. That same year the AFI became the first art institute to be included in the California Education Facilities Authority Pooled Bond Program, which infused the institute with $6.7 million from the tax-free bond issue to refinance the acquisition and renovation of the campus.

AFI raises awareness of the moving image as an art form within the creative community and with the wider American public through a multitude of national events and programs. AFI pursues this mission through its many exhibitions and by rewarding excellence in the field of the moving image, including:

AFI Life Achievement Award

Universally considered the most prestigious award given in honor of a career in film, the annual AFI Life Achievement Award is well-known to the American public through its broadcast each year on national television. Past recipients include John Ford, Lillian Gish, Alfred Hitchcock, John Huston, Gene Kelly, Elizabeth Taylor, Sidney Poitier, Steven Spielberg, Clint Eastwood and in 1997, Martin Scorsese.

AFI Los Angeles
International Film Festival

In 1996, the two-week festival attracted more than 40,000 people and was held in historic Hollywood. Highlights of the festival included a world premiere presentation of the recently discovered 1912 Richard III, *tributes to Anjelica Huston, Gena Rowlands and Louis Malle, an all-night movie marathon and a Tribute to Contemporary Mexican Cinema. Entering its 11th year, the festival is one of the most diverse film events in the United States, bringing top independent and foreign language films to Los Angeles.*

AFI Theater in Washington, D.C.

AFI also offers programs at the AFI Theater in the John F. Kennedy Center for the Performing Arts in Washington, D.C. Serving as a "national cinematheque," the AFI Theater is open to the public, offering more than 800 annual screenings, retrospectives, thematic series, tributes, and festival presentations.

One of the cornerstones of AFI's mission is the preservation of America's film, television and video heritage. Many of the moving images that are part of the collective memory of the 20th century are already lost or in danger of vanishing. Of the more than 21,000 feature-length films produced in the U.S. before 1951, only half exist today. AFI's preservation efforts—considered among the best in the world—work to protect our nation's moving image heritage. In 1996, AFI made international news with the historic discovery of the oldest surviving American feature film, a 1912 silent film version of *Richard III*, directed by James Keane and starring Frederick Warde.

Since 1991, AFI has played a leadership role in redefining the moving image in the era of the digital revolution by providing a unique environment for creative artists and technical visionaries to better understand and adapt to the future of visual communications. The institute has brought hundreds of high-technology companies, products, and leaders into direct contact with the creative community through a range of programs, exhibitions, conferences, seminars, hands-on training, and other related activities. AFI recently launched the AFI OnLine Cinema, making history by releasing classic films for the first time on the Internet.

Preserving, training, and celebrating, for thirty years the American Film Institute has sought to fulfill its mandate to support this greatest of American art forms, the art of the moving image.

Introduction

I used to work in live theater, where performers often regale each other with variations of the classic "Actor's Nightmare." They describe the horrifying sensation of finding themselves on stage, midperformance, and suddenly having no idea what play they're supposed to perform! They all react differently in their panic; some ramble, some freeze, and some simply run screaming from the stage. Then—thank heavens!—they wake up and realize the agony is only in their imagination. The nightmare is only a dream.

Now I work in Hollywood, where I discovered that there is also a "Screenwriter's Nightmare." It usually goes something like this:

> *You get a great idea for a script. You're eager, excited, and convinced that it will make a great movie. You jot down ideas that come easily at first, but eventually you begin to slow down. Something's wrong. What should you do? Ignore the sensation? Start over again?*

Often what happens is that you turn to the plethora of books or seminars available, where you're quickly assured that there are specific formulas that work for any script. Just put "these" events into "that" order and, voila, you've got yourself a hit screenplay! So you sit yourself back at the keyboard, happily convinced that the worst is behind you.

Usually it's not. Somehow the one-size-fits-all formulas don't fit your ideas, and the foolproof systems manage to fail. Panic, frustration, even paralysis set in. Now what do you do? Toss out your idea or abandon the formula? Give up on your script or trudge wearily to the end? Either way, you're unhappy with the outcome and never really sure whether the problem is your idea, your technique, your discipline, or simply a complete and utter lack of talent.

Wouldn't it be great if you woke up and found out it was all a bad dream? However, chances are you won't, because unlike the Actor's Nightmare, this one happens all the time.

I should know. I've been teaching screenwriting for several years now, and everywhere I go I meet talented but discouraged writers who are confused, frustrated, and even angry. They're tired of being taught rules that sound good but prove to be of little practical use. They're fed up with conventional wisdom that makes even the process of writing unsatisfying, while still not resulting in the professional success they crave.

Meanwhile, I've worked with hundreds of executives, producers, and directors who grow more and more alarmed at the difficulty of finding exciting, compelling screenplays. Each weekend they drag home piles of scripts searching for the next great hit, only to read material that seems so predictable it almost feels as if it's been cloned.

The problem is not just that formulaic writing makes for boring reading, but for boring films and television as well. "Hollywood is starving for good material!" screams one trade paper article after another, while box office slumps and TV ratings declines suggest that audiences agree. Yet scripts that follow such formulas continue to cross my desk by the hundreds each year. If the rules and conventions are so effective, why are so many scripts disappointing? Why do most screenplays fail?

Because the formulaic approach doesn't work. After reading more than 10,000 scripts over the course of my career, I can tell you categorically that there are no specifics that work for every screenplay. What is true, however, is that there are fundamental emotional and logical processes that audiences employ to make sense of any story. There is also a crucial relationship between those audience dynamics and the components of a screenplay. Once you understand those dynamics, you can begin to use craft imaginatively to express your unique vision rather than as a mold into which you must force your ideas.

That's why I decided to write this book. It's based on the course I teach at the American Film Institute's Center for Advanced Film and Television Studies. It is the result of my experience during more than twenty years in film, television, and theater. In this book we're going to take a different approach to screenwriting, one that is not only more exciting, satisfying, and productive but more commercially viable as well.

Anyone who's noticed how thick TV guides are becoming can see how rapidly entertainment choices are increasing. Thirty years ago there were three television channels and one Hollywood studio film playing in local movie theaters. Now we are careening through a futuristic world with hundreds of TV channels, while independent films are becoming a powerful force within the movie industry. As pay-per-view and video-on-demand become the norm and the foreign markets become the decisive factor in box office success, anyone who thinks that the simplistic formulas developed decades ago are still the only way to tell a story is missing the most important factor in the entertainment field today: Diversity, uniqueness, and individuality of vision is the only way to stand out in the chaotic and over-crowded marketplace.

Consider the splash made by Quentin Tarantino's *Pulp Fiction,* or the impressive careers of filmmakers like the Coen brothers or Oliver Stone. Consider the impact made when "The Simpsons," "Roseanne," or Tim Allen's "Home Improvement" joined the TV lineup. Meanwhile, many professionals expect independent and foreign films to dominate the 1997 Oscars. All these success stories signal that the most viable strategy for commercial success is to have a unique voice which expresses a world view we haven't heard before but recognize as true.

So rather than assuming that all successful screenplays contain specific contents that never vary, we'll approach cinematic storytelling as we would if you wanted to become a great architect. Every building employs the same basic physical dynamics. What you need to develop is not one blue print that you use for every assignment, but rather a deep, visceral appreciation of each component's inherent qualities and what function it performs. That way you can select exactly the right materials, techniques, and proportions for each building in order to bring your unique creations to life.

In this book we're going to focus on the components of a script. We'll go back to the very essence of the storytelling process and figure out for ourselves what sensations make a story experience satisfying for the audience, and how those dynamics are created. What are the fundamental elements of cinematic storytelling? How do they function, and how do they interact?

The dynamics we're going to explore are true for any form of screenwriting, whether you want to write for features, network TV, or cable. We'll begin with an in-depth discussion of "whys" before we start exploring the "hows," to bring both the internal and external challenges of screenwriting to your conscious awareness. The goal is to help you develop an "educated gut," which means having clear access to your creative instincts as well as the craft to express your story effectively.

So if you've suffered through the dreaded Screenwriter's Nightmare, it's time to wake up! Whether you want to write a zany comic escapade, an explosive action/adventure, or a quiet, poignant drama, this book can give you back the passion, clarity, and confidence needed to bring your cinematic dreams to life.

Films as Roller Coasters

You sit down. The room goes dark. You switch to the right channel on your TV or find your seat just before the film begins. The level of your involvement may start at "ground zero," but if something about the story catches your interest, you soon become curious. Even better, if something about the story touches you emotionally, you get hooked. If the story continues to work its magic, your overall pattern of anticipation and emotional investment becomes more and more intense. Your heart may pound as the climax approaches, soaring with hope or plummeting with despair when the story ends. But however the story resolves itself, if it has held your interest and provoked strong emotions, the end result is that your internal tension subsides, and the experience leaves you spent, but satisfied, in a pleasurable and almost physical way.

Isn't that what it feels like to watch a wonderful movie or something great on TV? Wouldn't you love to write screenplays that provoke such compelling sensations in your audience?

Creating that kind of emotional reaction is the great challenge of screenwriting. However, the screenwriting approaches that have become popular over the last decades may handicap you. They focus your attention on determining your story's logical sequence of events, rather than on how to create emotional impact. Such methods are often conveyed by linear diagrams indicating a "correct" order of plot events. Some approaches even indicate what sequence, or by which page number, key plot events should occur.

Not only do I believe such linear prototypes are an inaccurate depiction of the ideal story experience, I think such images actually work against your chance of creating a compelling screenplay. The reason is that while designing a logically cohesive plotline is certainly part of writing a great screenplay, focusing exclusively on the rational progression of events is too one dimensional to create the results you want. Logic and emotions are two different things. A well-constructed legal argument can be dry as dust, while a rambling and almost incoherent mother can break your heart as she tries to explain the accident that killed her child.

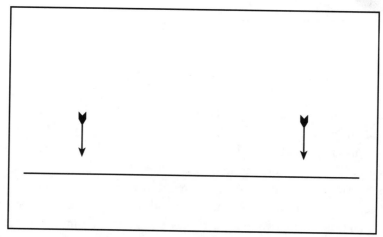

Figure 1-1   Linear Structure with Key Moments

So you must focus on creating a compelling emotional build of tension and release in your story. It is that overall experience for which audiences hunger, and which will ultimately determine whether your story will be emotionally satisfying or not.

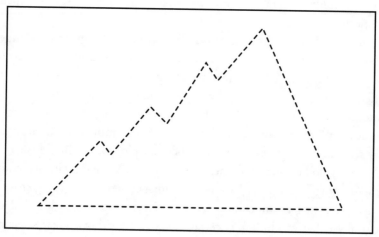

Figure 1-2   Two-Dimensional Roller Coaster

As a result, rather than thinking of your cinematic story as a linear construction (as in Figure 1-1), I suggest that you begin thinking of it as a two-dimensional roller coaster (as in Figure 1-2).

In terms of the cinematic experience, what is going on here? What information is being conveyed here? What exactly do these two lines represent?

The bottom line reflects the rational, logical progression of plot information, while the upper line suggests the resulting emotional reaction you want viewers to have. For example, when the story begins, viewers start at a neutral emotional level because they have no information about the plot. Their interest will remain at this level until at least one aspect of the story provokes some curiosity; then, if the story begins to intrigue them, the intensity of their emotional reaction begins to build. The more their emotions are aroused, the more eager they are to know what's going to happen. Maybe a surprise suddenly spurs their interest, or a slow, gentle scene allows them to feel a momentary sense of calm, but the overall pattern of their emotional reaction continues to rise higher and higher. Finally it climaxes; then internal tension begins to subside.

There are several reasons I like the roller-coaster analogy. One is that it captures the sense of thrust, power, build, and intensity that a good story experience must have. Suddenly it's not enough to decide what will be the next major event in your story. You also need to ask yourself, "How do I make this scene intense enough to create the height I need for this portion of my story roller coaster?" Envisioning the intended highs and lows of your story as the two-dimensional visual image of a roller coaster will give focus and clarity to your creative goals.

Most important, the roller-coaster image graphically conveys the first big secret of successful screenwriting. The cinematic story experience is not just composed of the words you put on the paper (or the resulting sights and sounds that may end up on the screen one day), but also the audience's emotional reaction to that information. Your goal is to write screenplays that provide such a compelling pattern of emotional highs and lows that anyone reading your script can easily imagine an audience also enjoying the cinematic ride.

Story roller coasters are composed of five major elements—structure, plot, characters, momentum, and style. Each of these will be examined in more detail in later chapters, but here is a quick overview to give you a sense of these five core components, how they function, and how they interact.

I. Structure

The first and most prominent component of a screenplay is *structure*, the overall design or track of the roller coaster. The function of structure is to provide the comprehensive, "big picture" ride that determines whether your audience will experience a satisfying build to climax and release.

The easiest way to understand structure is to imagine it as the pattern or design of emotional ups and downs that the audience experiences while watching your story. It's almost as if you could hook up EKGs to the bodies of your viewers; when they feel an intense emotion the needle will leap up and when they become bored the needle will descend. By the end of the story, the graph will reflect the exact shape of their emotional reaction. That resulting pattern is what's represented by the roller coaster's design, which is the structure of your story.

The generic version of the cinematic roller coaster (Figure 1-3) can be represented by a simple triangle that is the essential shape of any good story. This graph reflects the audience's neutral emotional involvement at the start, which then builds to climax and release.

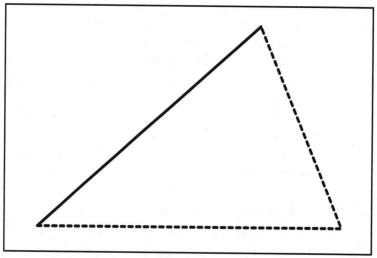

Figure 1-3   Generic Roller Coaster

However, most stories are not constructed in such a linear way. For example, Figure 1-4 shows a kind of "meandering grapevine" roller coaster from a character piece like *A Room With a View:*

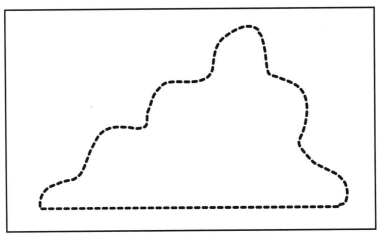

Figure 1-4   Meandering Roller Coaster

In contrast, some stories are built so that a plot twist suddenly piques the audience's interest, or a slow, peaceful interlude is inserted to give them a breather before the next build begins. Figure 1-5 shows the jagged roller coaster of an exciting, event-filled horror film such as *Hellraiser* or *Nightmare on Elm Street:*

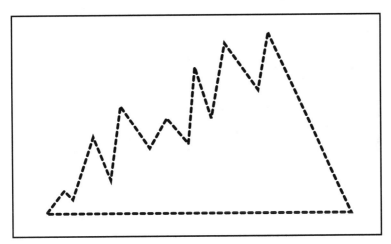

Figure 1-5   Jagged Roller Coaster

Figure 1-6 illustrates the roller coaster of a low-jeopardy mystery such as "Matlock" or "Murder, She Wrote", which reflects the audience's less emotional, more logical, stair-step reaction to possible clues:

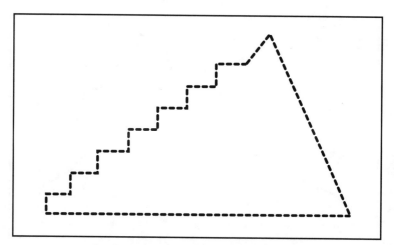

Figure 1-6   Stair Step Roller Coaster

Although a successful structure must end with a climactic build, it doesn't always have to begin slowly. Some films, such as *The Fugitive,* start with a big bang, after which the tensions descend before they begin to rebuild. That kind of structure would be represented by Figure 1-7.

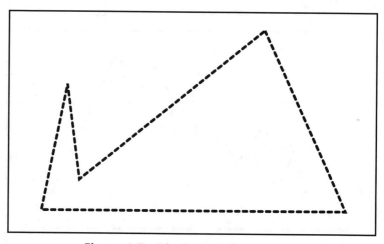

Figure 1-7   Big Bang Roller Coaster

The point is that since the structure of your story reflects the pattern of the audience's reactions, you can build whatever shape roller coaster you think will most effectively convey your story. The only constant is that the overall build must eventually achieve an effective climax and resolution. It is this big picture pattern which allows the audience to have the satisfaction of a real catharsis.

II. Plot

Once you have a sense of what kind of roller coaster you want to build, how exactly do you go about building it? Often the next step is to develop and arrange the *plot,* whose function is to convey a sequence of events that evokes the desired pattern of emotional highs and lows in the audience. In that sense, the audience's emotional reaction to a series of individual plot points is what creates the overall structure, or story roller coaster you have designed.

I like to refer to story points as story "pillars" because the height of a story "pillar" reflects the intensity of the audience's emotional reaction to that piece of plot information. For example, if you were dramatizing the following story, you might decide to begin building your roller coaster by giving the audience four key pieces of information:

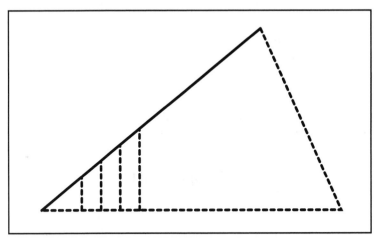

Figure 1-8   Ascending Story Pillars

In this example, you are building your structure based on the assumption that viewers will care a little bit when they learn that the heroine is a married woman who has just become pregnant. They will care a little more when they learn that she's already suffered three miscarriages, more when the doctor says she may have cancer, and even more when she goes home to her drunken spouse who pushes her down the stairs.

Not all stories have to be dramatic, of course; they don't even have to be serious. A story pillar can be built by any kind of emotion—laughter, fear, excitement, or rage. It's the intensity of the audience's reaction that determines a pillar's height, and it's the height that supports the story's structure. As the story progresses, at least some of the pillars must rise higher and higher in order to build to an effective climax and release. No matter what roller coaster pattern you choose, the overall structure is ultimately supported by the audience's reaction to each individual pillar.

For the audience, the dynamic of a successful story pillar is reminiscent of the game played at state fairs in which people try to force a heavy metal clanger up a vertical pole by hitting the launcher with a sledgehammer. The sensation created in the audience when a pillar "hits the bell" is almost physical. For instance, remember the first time you saw *Body Heat?* During the final third of the film nearly every scene created that visceral "click" as the emotional stakes pushed higher and higher, and the sensation felt almost like a series of small internal explosions. Creating that sense of "hitting the bell" in an audience requires an accurate understanding of how viewers will react to the new information. Keeping the viewers in mind as you polish your script can help you select and arrange the story information that creates the intended pattern of highs and lows.

Because of the intricate relationship between plot and structure, many people get them confused. Just remember that your plot is the selection and arrangement of story events. Structure is the overall pattern created by your audience's emotional reaction to that information.

III. Characters

Characters are the next major component of a cinematic roller coaster. Their function is to lure your viewers "on board." After all, it's one thing to watch a roller coaster from a safe distance. It's an entirely different experience to actually get on and take the ride!

Characters fulfill this function by provoking a strong sense of recognition in viewers. Ideally, audience members feel as though at least one character is their emotional "proxy," representing some key aspect of their lives. That commonality may be found in the characters' actions, their motives, or in their emotional reactions to events. What's important is that the characters somehow mirror the audience's own experience, longings, or fantasies. Once that bond occurs, viewers feel as though the events of the story were happening to them, thus intensifying the emotional impact of the plot.

Unlike some approaches that insist all heroes and heroines function the same way in any story, I believe there are various kinds of heroes that evoke different emotional connections to viewers. The obvious differences between popular heroes like James Bond, Forrest Gump, Citizen Kane, or TV's Roseanne are based on the very distinct kinds of emotional connection you need to understand so you can develop genuine "rooting interest."

Similarly, the spectrum of antagonists, from the terrifying killer of *The Terminator* to the humorous, mischievous *Dennis the Menace*, also reflect a variety of ways audience members view the opponents and obstacles in their own lives. Secondary characters are most successfully used when they separate and intensify the differences between heroes and the world around them.

IV. Momentum

The next element in constructing a roller coaster is *momentum*, the internal forward thrust created when viewers become eager, even anxious, to see what will happen next. This is the power that drives the story through to completion. Momentum is the engine that powers the roller coaster, and its function is to keep the cars moving so that the viewers never have an opportunity to get off. Without momentum, you could design the world's most impressive roller coaster and even manage to get viewers on board, but the cars would just sit there.

To create eagerness in the audience, the screenwriter intentionally plants questions in the viewers' minds—almost like leaving a trail of bread crumbs in a forest. You guide and focus your viewers' attention by the way you give and withhold information. Viewers can then experience a sense of satisfaction when they finally get the answer for which they've been searching.

Audiences experience a sense of momentum when they become eager to know both how the logical elements will come together and what the emotional ramifications of those events will be. The audience's hunger for information should grow progressively stronger as the story develops, intensifying the impact of the plot and the emotional connection with characters. Television shows like "The X-Files" and movies like *No Way Out* achieve a lot of their power by cleverly introducing clues and questions that leave viewers eager to get the answer.

V. Style

The final component of a roller coaster is *style,* whose function is to intensify the key sensations of the ride, those that best convey the essence of your story.

Writers often think of style as an optional decoration that can be applied like a few last-minute curlicues painted on the side of roller-coaster cars. However, it is much more like the difference between riding on a modern, well-greased track that magnifies every twist and turn, or lurching along on an old, wobbly contraption that feels as if it's going to come to a stop at any moment.

The reason style is so important is that it's virtually omnipresent in the audience's awareness. Long before people in the audience know if they're interested in your characters, or if the plot will hold their interest, they have a strong sense of your style.

The reason is that style is reflected in every line of dialogue or stage description in your script, and conveys much of your individual "voice" as a writer. For example, if you read the first five pages of *Pulp Fiction* and *The Piano,* you would immediately sense the differences between the two writers even if you knew nothing of the overall stories.

Yet because screenwriters realize that they don't have all the stylistic tools available to filmmakers, many abdicate this area of choice completely, or allow it to happen without regard for how it impacts their story. They underestimate the profound impact and power of the style choices they *do* have at their disposal.

The conscious and creative use of concise, well-chosen words can evoke powerful images, sensations, pace, and tone that can dramatically enhance your script. Style can intensify important aspects of your plot, characters, and momentum, which can make the overall roller coaster ride unified. However, never forget that style functions as an intensifier, so it's important that you use it to enhance the viewers' experience, rather than to add random decorative flourishes that can distract from the cohesiveness of the overall ride.

■ Creating a Great Roller Coaster ■

Because elements of roller coasters can be combined in an almost endless variety, writers have great freedom in constructing their cinematic stories, as you can see in such disparate films as *Babe, Natural Born Killers, Ed Wood,*

Airplane, and *Shine,* or TV series like "Married . . . With Children" and "Law And Order." Yet there are some aspects of the story experience that never change, so let's discuss those in Chapter Two.

Q U E S T I O N S

The more you can begin to recognize each component of a story roller coaster, the more you will identify its contribution to the overall ride. Ask yourself these questions to help identify specific elements in the movies and TV shows you've seen:

1. Which movies and TV shows have given you the most compelling roller-coaster rides?

2. How would you graph the structure of your three favorite movies? TV shows?

3. What kinds of roller coasters do you find most exciting as an audience member?
     Are those the same kinds of cinematic roller coasters you try to build as a writer?

4. Have you ever gotten "on board" with a compelling character?

5. Which characters affected you this way?
     What aspect of your hopes or fears did those characters represent?

6. Can you think of cinematic stories that provoked a strong sense of momentum?
     What questions did they make you ask?
     Did the story answer them?

7. How does your inner experience differ when there is a strong sense of momentum and when there's not?

8. Which movies have used style effectively for you? Which TV shows?

9. Which movies and TV shows have lacked the sense of style they needed?

10. Which stories have had the best balance of all the above elements?
     What is the connection between that list and the list of your favorite films?

11. Do these same story dynamics work as well for you on television shows?

    Why or why not?

12. What's the connection between your favorite shows and how well these elements work?

    What about your least favorite shows?

How Do Roller Coasters Work?

If story roller coasters can be so varied, how can there be any constants? What, if anything, do such diverse roller coasters as those for *Ace Ventura, JFK, The Secret Garden, The Relic, Das Boot (The Boat), Twelve Monkeys,* and *Driving Miss Daisy* have in common?

There are some constants that you must learn to recognize in order to create a compelling roller coaster ride for your audience. However, they're not in the external elements of the roller coaster design. They reside in the internal processes that viewers experience as they ride your roller coaster and try to make sense of both the emotional and logical contents of the story.

These internal audience processes are rarely discussed, perhaps because they are usually experienced at a subconscious level. However, just because the average audience member cannot articulate them doesn't mean they aren't important. The truth is that they dominate the audience's subjective experience as they watch your story, so it's crucial that you know how they operate.

Identifying the mental and emotional needs an audience brings to a story may seem a bit difficult at first because they usually exist on the subconscious level; but they are not irrational, arbitrary, or unpredictable. One good way to watch how they operate is to observe yourself when you watch a film or read a script. No matter how long you've been writing, chances are that you've spent hundreds or even thousands more hours as an audience member than as a writer. Watching your own process gives you a chance to become conscious of how other people react to stories. The more you pay attention to your own internal processes, the more you will see that both the logic-based questions and emotional reactions are amazingly consistent. The more conscious you become of them, the more clearly you will understand the power of the emotional and intellectual energy you, as a screenwriter, are trying to harness and convey.

Before considering formulas or screenwriting itself, let's go back to the core human dynamics that create the hunger for stories. Throughout most of this book we will be concentrating on techniques of writing for the screen, but first we need to go back to the very foundation of storytelling. Let's find out what an audience wants from a story and why, before we start discussing the "hows" of making successful emotional contact with your viewers.

■ Back to the Beginning ■

Humanity has gathered to hear stories since the earliest known societies, but people still haven't had their fill. The storytelling technologies change, but the fundamental urges that drive people to sit at the "story hearth" are as strong today as they were for cave dwellers thousands of years ago. Why do audiences want stories? What sensations do they get? Why are those sensations appealing?

Audiences like stories because stories give them emotional experiences they often can't have in real life. Just as riding a real roller coaster gives people an opportunity to enjoy experiences that are more exciting than their everyday lives, a captivating story roller coaster provokes the same sense of exhilaration that makes audiences feel truly alive.

Yet most stories are entirely fictional and even those based on fact are still somewhat artificial, so why should a fictionalized story event have such emotional impact on audiences? How can emotions provoked by such an artificial medium be so compelling?

The reason is that people think in stories. Dreams, worries, gossip, religion, myths, and science are all stories that humans have created to give some sense of order and meaning to their lives that they can't always find in everyday experiences. The process of creating stories is so universal that some scientists now speculate that it was this ability, rather than the use of tools, which began to separate humans from other primates. Meanwhile, the inability to string pieces of information into a coherent sequence is the universal definition of insane.

Yet the mental process of piecing together a jigsaw puzzle, while stimulating to our logical mind, provokes a very different sensation from experiencing a satisfying story. In order to be emotionally involving, the pieces of the story eventually have to become personally meaningful, and the more direct the connection, the more power the story has.

▪ Getting Away From It All ▪

The entertainment industry has long known that viewers are eager to escape the frustrations of everyday life, so there has been a lot of emphasis on topics and characters that provide fantasy fulfillment. TV shows like "Baywatch" or movies like *Pretty Woman* and *Goldeneye* are specifically calculated to take the viewer into a fantasy world of glamour, youth, sexuality, or power.

But there are much deeper emotional needs that people bring to the story experience. These come from the desire to find relief from the frustrations at the core of the internal human experience. These internal quandaries are the same for all people, no matter how different their external circumstances are. These are hidden deep in the psyche so people are rarely conscious of them. Yet it is the mounting hunger for these four emotional states that drive the audience's energies toward the story's climax, while having these needs fully addressed is what provides the final sense of satisfaction and release.

An audience's ability to become involved with your story exists in direct proportion to how much that story satisfies those needs. So you must be conscious of what they are and recognize the connection between these hungers and the function of each component of a story roller coaster.

So what kinds of emotional needs do people bring to a story? When we talk about stories being emotionally satisfying, what do we mean? Let's first explore the four fundamentals that all humans crave from the story experience. Then we will examine the logical process that the human mind employs in order to get those emotional needs met.

The Four Emotional Needs

1. The Need for New Information

Humans are constantly in a push/pull, love/hate relationship between their desire for new experience and their anxiety about its possible negative consequences. Sometimes referred to as the "neophile/neophobe" conflict (love of the new/fear of the new), most people shuttle back and forth between wanting new stimulation and fearing the consequences of new stimulation every day of their lives.

For example, until a hundred years ago, most people never ventured more than a few miles away from where they were born. Imagine how well they got to know those few miles, and how they must have longed to see what was over the next mountain or beyond the seashore. Yet perhaps they lived in a time when people thought that monsters lurked in the next valley or that the world was flat. They faced the choice of staying home and safe, or getting answers to their questions by risking their lives. Even today, when modem technology has made physical boundaries less daunting, people are still torn between their desire to engage in new activities and their reluctance to take risks.

Stories are an ideal way to address this hunger. One of the great things about riding a real roller coaster is that while passengers feel as though they are hurtling through space, they are actually quite safe. Stories also let audience members experience fascinating new sensations without having to take real-life risks.

Most people's imaginations are filled with hundreds of adventures they would love to experience, but that simply aren't possible in everyday life. Therefore stories that promise to provide such new sensations attract viewers. *Top Gun* gave audiences a taste of being a fighter pilot, while *The Player* conveyed a sense of what it must feel like to be a Hollywood big shot. Intriguing settings, new sensations, or unknown worlds (whether it's another planet or a behind-the-scenes glimpse of a more familiar world) promise novelty. This enhances a screenplay's appeal by taking viewers into other worlds and experiences they may never have on their own.

Satisfying the audience's hunger for new information is often a function fulfilled by the basic concept or control idea of the story, but every component of a roller coaster can contain such appeal. Unique characters, unusual momentum devices, and original use of style all have the ability to satisfy the audience's hunger for new stimuli.

2. The Need to Bond

Have you ever taken a wild amusement park ride and been stuck sitting with a stranger? At first you may feel uncomfortable, but after you spend a few minutes screaming together or hanging on for dear life, you walk away feeling a real, if temporary, sense of closeness with that person. That's the experience audience members can have if they are able to feel a sense of connection and commonality during a story, either with the characters on the screen or with other members of the audience.

In real life, humans can never really know what others are thinking and feeling, no matter how close they are. In fact, one respected psychologist claims that most people will have only thirteen minutes of genuine intimacy in their entire lives. Only during those few precious minutes of complete emotional bonding will they feel no sense of separation between themselves and others. Thus the hunger to bond is constant and profound, because humans live in an internal world of constant, if unconscious, isolation.

Not only can it be lonely to feel such persistent emotional separation, but according to some, it can also be dangerous. Charles Darwin believed that animals who were isolated from their social group were more vulnerable, because they had no opportunity to learn which emotions to value and act on and which to dismiss. For instance, a young monkey who isn't taught to run away in fear at the sound of a crashing branch may be killed. As a result, Darwin considered a species' ability to synchronize emotions crucial to survival.

That's why people have a great need to have their emotions expressed and affirmed by stories. Watching someone in a story express the same emotions they experience tells people they are not crazy, and that they are not alone. In a story, audiences can "get inside" characters for long stretches of time, and the more time spent bonded with a character, the more satisfying the story experience.

Thus the need for humans to experience emotional bonds, which affirm their inner experience and help them feel connected to the outside world, is a driving, compelling hunger. One of the main reasons people watch films is to satisfy that urge, and if a film is successful, the sense of total envelopment helps people achieve catharsis. *Elephant Man* is a film that had that kind of impact on me; students in my class have mentioned *Shine, E.T.,* and *Platoon,* among others, as films that have affected them in that way.

Characters are usually the component of the roller coaster that allows viewers to bond with a story. By exploring characters' thoughts, actions, motives, and dreams, the audience has a chance to recognize deeper personal truths, even if they've never lived through that specific situation. However, audiences can also bond through plot events that are related to their own lives, momentum devices that pull them into the story, and stylistic elements that make them feel as though they are experiencing the events on the screen firsthand.

3. The Need for Conflict Resolution

Another emotional hunger drawing people to stories is the need to learn more about how to resolve problems, how to deal with conflict and change, and how to take appropriate action. Many people avoid these in real life due to the possible negative consequences, so they live in constant vigilance against their own emotions such as anger or resentment of injustice. Yet it takes a great deal of energy to constantly hold in emotions, so people develop a strong need to "act" vicariously on such conflicts as a way of venting the emotional pressure inside their own heads.

A real roller coaster provides riders with a sense of "triumph" at the end for surviving each exciting twist and turn, even though they were really just passive observers. Story roller coasters offer a similar sensation—the audience can vicariously explore what it's like to act in confrontations and face grave danger without paying the price.

Audiences like stories that help them understand how to face and triumph over conflict, whether it's physical, as in *Cliffhanger,* or emotional, as in *Ordinary People.* The plot is the element of stories that deals with this; it offers an opportunity to handle change and conflict vicariously, by providing role models, warnings, lessons, and encouragement that can help viewers deal with their everyday lives. However, conflict resolution can also be addressed in provocative characterizations, momentum devices that make audiences struggle to put together the pieces of the puzzle, and stylistic elements that intensify the sense of danger and risk.

4. The Need for Completion

The last great need for which people come to stories derives from the fact that humans are forced to live their entire lives lacking full knowledge about almost everything. Yet they must make decisions and take action every day. The constant effort to act despite incomplete information is, at the least, very tiring and sometimes profoundly disturbing. Consequently, one of the strongest desires people have is to take a vacation from the gnawing sense of uncertainty. They long to spend time in a world where issues will be resolved and questions will be answered.

That's why stories that convey the promise of completion and order are the most satisfying, because these are exactly the sensations that people can't usually find in real life. When they ride a real roller coaster, people feel as though they are experiencing random twists and turns. Yet they know that the cars will eventually come to a halt, and their climactic build of tension will end with a powerful sense of relaxation and relief. Story roller coasters constructed to give riders the confidence that "all will be revealed" have a tremendous appeal that has as much to do with the way a story is told as with the topic itself.

Viewers are willing to undergo extended periods of suspense and mystery as long as the questions are answered by the end. For example, "Twin Peaks" was a fabulous experiment in television. Its style, sensibility, characterizations, and world view were absolutely captivating. It was only in the area of promising completion that it eventually failed, yet that was enough to drive viewers away once they lost faith that their most central questions would be answered.

Momentum is the aspect of a story that promises the audience completion by providing a satisfying pattern of mental "questions and answers" which viewers experience as they move through a story. The sense of completion can also be conveyed in plots that are logically coherent, character arcs that seem convincing, and stylistic choices that intensify the key moments of discovery as viewers put together the pieces of the story puzzle.

The Five Mental Processes

If humans are so eager to have these emotional needs met through stories, then why do so many stories fail?

Despite the intensity of our emotional needs, the logical processes we use to absorb story information are very complex. The analytical nature of our brains can distract us from becoming emotionally absorbed, unless a story addresses our logical concerns as well. Therefore, in addition to the four emotional hungers, you also need to understand the five mental processes audiences employ to make sense out of any story:

1. Resistance

Often writers assume that the audience is totally open to the storytelling experience simply because they have purchased tickets or turned on the TV. However, viewers actually experience a strong sense of initial resistance that you need to understand in order to overcome it.

To understand this resistance, imagine sitting in a room where a movie screen suddenly drops down and the lights begin to dim. Wouldn't you feel an immediate sense of tension? "Will this be boring?" "Will I enjoy it?" "Will I be able to get out if I want to leave?" The more cinematically literate our society becomes, the harder it is to get audiences to open up and give themselves completely to the storytelling experience. Too many times, movies that are supposed to be great turn out to be duds, and the new hit television shows are a bore.

One way Hollywood has tried to solve this is by encouraging writers to create big openings in the first ten pages. There should be something compelling to capture the audience's attention, but a big action scene isn't the only way to do it. Once you understand the dynamic you are trying to create, you can choose from hundreds of ways to get the audience involved in your story. You can lure them, charm them, shock them, amuse them, make them curious, or create practically any other compelling emotion, as long as it works within the overall unity of your story.

2. Need for Orientation

As viewers try to make sense of your story, their minds start looking for landmarks that they can use to orient themselves. "Who is this character?" "Why are they in this building?" "What are they doing?" Viewers' minds are searching for clues, so, in that sense, every story is a mystery, no matter what its genre.

Therefore, storytelling styles that give clear emphasis to key information help minimize confusion and distraction. The faster viewers can figure out what and who is important in a story, the sooner they can begin to understand the emotional significance of events. That allows their own subjective roller-coaster experience to begin to climb.

3. Expanding from Landmarks

Once viewers begin to feel oriented, they start to build on that knowledge by deciding which pieces of new information seem pertinent to what they've already concluded is important. Each piece of information they think is important becomes a dot; then they try to connect the dots and tell the best possible story from the available information.

You must make sure that you are aware of what the key information is. Then you can clearly convey it to viewers so that they experience the same roller coaster you intended to build.

4. Assessing the Effort

If viewers are able to assemble the pieces quickly and easily, they feel encouraged to become more emotionally involved. If the pieces are hard to put together, the effort involved can really drag down an audience's enthusiasm for the story.

Recent studies of how people respond to music indicate that the ease with which audiences can create a meaningful pattern is a major source of their enjoyment. Making sense out of dissonant, progressive jazz, for example, is hard, and many people will eventually withdraw from the experience because the pleasure they are deriving isn't worth the effort it takes.

The same is true of people's involvement in a story. If the ratio between an audience's moment-to-moment efforts and satisfaction becomes too lopsided, the audience will start to lose interest. Their consciousness of the "unrequited" effort makes them feel vulnerable in a manner which most viewers don't like. If obtaining the information becomes too difficult, or if too much useless information is obtained, viewers will eventually feel alienated from the story.

5. Continuous Decision-Making

Often writers mistakenly assume that the audience's assessment of whether or not the story experience was worthwhile only comes at the end of the story. However, studies have shown that the audience is actually constantly making decisions; this is reflected in the moment-to-moment ups and downs seen in the story structure. Even if you are building a roller coaster that peaks in one climactic moment, you must still tell your story in a way that holds the viewers' logical and emotional interest from the first moment to the last.

Dealing with Negative Space

In Asian art, there are two kinds of energy in any painting. One is the "positive space," which is filled with the actual visible decorations such as paint, ink, or embroidery. The "negative space" is the portion that may look empty to Western eyes. However, the whole point of the positive/negative approach to art is to understand that there really is no empty space. Both aspects of the painting are crucial, and it is the balance and proportion between them that ultimately determines whether the artwork is effective.

The same is true for an audience's experience of a cinematic story. The positive space is the information that a writer actually writes on the page, or a filmmaker puts on the screen. The negative space contains all the audience's subjective thoughts and reactions that occur as they try to understand and process your "positive" story material.

All logical and emotional processes that viewers use to make sense of story material takes place in their negative space. If processing information and getting emotionally involved take too much effort, the viewer's internal awareness remains focused on the activity in their negative space, which distances them from your story.

The goal for a dramatist is to present the positive space with emotional appeal and logical clarity. This allows viewers' negative space, usually filled with the details and concerns of everyday life, to fade away, at least for a little while. This level of total involvement can only happen when both the audience's intellectual and emotional needs are met.

Just because the audience has these needs doesn't mean that you must address them immediately. Exciting sensations can be created for the audience when those hungers are postponed in an intriguing and tantalizing way. But your chances of meeting those needs decrease sharply if you're not even conscious that they exist. That's why understanding these core emotional and logical processes is so crucial.

The conventional rules of storytelling have evolved from efforts to meet these audience hungers, and often some have proven successful over time. The more writers use these now-familiar solutions, the more cliché and ineffectual they become. So one of the major challenges of being a successful storyteller is to find new ways to meet those age-old needs.

The way to write a great screenplay is to ignore the aging formulas and commit yourself to finding the specific solutions that best fit the needs of your roller coaster. The secret is not to rely on old conventional wisdom and rules, but really to understand the relationship between the "whys" and "hows" of creating a cinematic roller coaster. Then you will be free to break conventions whenever other choices are more suited to your story.

Now you have a sense of what an audience's internal process is. In the next chapter, we'll talk about the intellectual and emotional challenges of your own creative process that you must face in order to write the screenplay of your dreams.

As we go through this book, you will see again and again that it is these same story dynamics that are at the core of every aspect of storytelling. The more viscerally you are aware of your own internal processes, the more you can understand exactly what emotional and intellectual reactions you are trying to evoke from your audience. Think about the last time you saw a movie:

1. What did you feel when the movie began?
   When did you feel the first sense of excitement?

2. What questions did you find yourself asking?
   How easy was it for you to find the answers?
   What reactions did you have if the movie answered them effectively?
   What reactions did you have if it didn't?

3. If you ultimately decided the film was bad, when did you realize it?
   What made you first suspect this? Why?
   When were you sure?
   How did you feel when you reached your conclusion?

4. What happened if you thought the film was good?

5. What kinds of activities were going on in your negative space?
   Were they enhancing your enjoyment of the movie, or were they distracting?

6. When you got bored, how dominant did your negative space become?
   When you were really involved, how dominant was it?

7. Were you more aware of the positive space or the negative space as the movie progressed?
   How did that correlate with your overall enjoyment of the film?

8. Which was the strongest attraction in the film for you . . .
   New stimulation?
   Bonding?
   Conflict resolution?
   Promise of completeness?

9. What films are your favorites?
   What lured you onto those roller coasters?
   Which of the four hungers did those stories most appeal to?

10. Have you ever felt total catharsis in a film?
    How many of the hungers did that film fulfill for you?

Creativity: The Building Process

I used to think that the hardest part of the creative process was dealing with the reactions from the outside world. But the more writers I meet, the more I realize the biggest obstacle is often the internal sense of confusion, indecision, and doubt that can plague the creative mind during the writing process. Therefore, before we continue discussing the aspects of a successful story roller coaster, let's examine the core creative process. Writers who find a dependable approach for dealing with creative challenges usually are able to continue writing long enough to become at least a modest success, while those who never master a method of overcoming such problems usually end up dropping out and never achieving their dreams.

Psychologists warn about the power of an unconscious belief; just because impulses aren't conscious doesn't mean they're not dominating your thinking, and I think this is particularly true for the creative process. In fact, the more unconscious the impulses are, the more they can control you, because you don't have a chance to use your logic or conscious willpower to counteract them. You need to bring the entire process up to the conscious level, which will dramatically increase your chances of finding the approach to screenwriting that works best for you.

I wish I could tell you that there is a simple, easy way to avoid this messy part of screenwriting, but the truth is that the creative process is messy—damn messy. There are very few writers I know who go through a story without some moments of feeling lost or confused. However, understanding how the creative process works can take away some of the fear. It will help you find an approach that works for you, allowing you to go deep into those dark interior woods confident that you can find your way out again.

So before we look at the technique of building a screenplay, let's look at the process of being creative. It's an area that's rarely examined, yet almost every problem encountered in screenwriting ultimately stems from misunderstanding its basic challenges.

The Creative Process

The creative process is an attempt to take intangible, often highly subjective ideas and emotions and convey them to the outside world. The creative urge is driven by the need to express the truth as the writer sees it. To do that successfully, a writer must get in touch with internal messages often stored deep in the psyche. The human brain makes subconscious associations between various ideas and/or objects, and many are very socially acceptable ways to "connect the dots." These are usually easy to access and unintimidating to express. For example, it's usually not too scary to expose your thoughts on current events or the type of music you like.

However, the core truths lie much deeper and it can be very frightening to reveal them. Humans make subjective, even irrational, connections based on their experiences, personalities, and observations. These provoke internal emotions that the outside world may not accept or understand, so people try to keep them hidden, even from themselves. Yet these same unique and private associations are the source of a writer's most powerful insights and authentic passions.

Things can become confusing at this stage because writers are often torn between two strong polarities. They want to express themselves, but they also want to avoid whatever psychological pain is involved in becoming conscious of inner truths. The two halves battle back and forth, and anyone who's ever gone through it knows how overwhelming the internal struggle can be. The core challenge of the creative process is to deal with the internal push/pull without losing clarity and focus, because the same search for inner truths that can shut writers down can also make their writing come alive.

The Creative Challenge

It's easy to get stuck in a tug-of-war between wanting to express yourself and wanting to hide your inner world. The mind can create very effective defense mechanisms, which complicate what would seem like a simple series of creative choices. Sometimes it happens when you're facing a major creative problem, other times it's only a minor concern; but suddenly your inability to find a solution can create paralyzing self-doubt. If the situation continues, doubts can evolve into fear—fear that you can't do justice to the idea, or even that it isn't worth doing justice to. You may try to fight the fear by ignoring it, plowing past uncertainties, or arguing with that voice in your head; yet those reactions rarely resolve the initial creative dilemma, and can drive you off course even further.

The worse the frustration becomes, the more you crave something certain, which is the appeal of writing according to a screenplay formula. Many writers are convinced that there is one right way to write. They cling to the seeming certainty of formulas, and every time they feel an impulse to stray from a formula, they ignore it, or decide it must be wrong, which cuts them off from the deepest source of their talent. Yet standardized rules rarely fit an individual story, so then they become even more confused. "What am I doing wrong?" "Why can't I figure this out?" "How can I be a good writer if these rules don't feel right to me?"

If you face this situation, you may feel lost and discouraged, and wonder if you've chosen a bad idea, or simply whether you lack talent. At this point the "pinball effect" begins. You start shuttling back and forth between allegiance to rules and disdain for formulas, losing sight of your original vision and getting bored by the familiarity of the choices that formulas encourage you to make. The longer the confusion goes on, the more distracting it becomes, forcing you to focus your creative energy on which approach you should use rather than on your screenplay.

The temptation is to change your idea in order to fit some predetermined mold. You begin denying your instincts and working more from your head, but your initial clarity also shifts as you move further and further away from your original vision. Some writers force themselves to trudge forward; others abandon any conscious use of craft, determined not to compromise the integrity of their story.

Initially the rejection of craft can seem very freeing, but ultimately it works no better than the formulaic approach. Depending only on instinctive choices can seem right one day and wrong the next, because those choices are based on momentary preference rather than a clear creative intention. You make changes and more changes, but it eventually becomes clear that you're just making your story different instead of better.

■ Craft vs. Creativity ■

The hidden premise of this thinking is that craft and creativity are mutually exclusive, so you must choose one approach or the other. Yet writers who abandon their instincts and writers who refuse to use craft are both making the same mistake. Using only one or the other is like trying to cross the ocean guided only by intuition, or staying in a cabin using only instruments and maps. To increase your chance of a safe crossing you need both, using one to double-check the other, because then you have the widest possible range of options no matter what problems occur.

The reason you need craft and creativity is that each serves a different function. Like the left-brain/right-brain interaction of the human mind, both have a vital place in the creative process. A successful screenplay must orchestrate the intellectual and emotional energies of the audience in order to fully engage their negative space. Therefore a great script needs the spark of creative passion and excitement that only inspiration can provide, as well as the clarity and logic that craft can ensure.

The right side of the brain helps you develop an instinctive sense of what you want your story to accomplish, while the left side helps determine which tools of the craft will best achieve that goal. Just as an architect must have a solid command of craft (although ultimate success will actually come from the ability to use it imaginatively), a good screenwriter must find the right balance between head and heart. You must dominate the tools and fundamentals of your craft, but ultimately your selection of how and why to use them should transcend simplistic formulas and rules and be inspired by your own, more personal, and more exciting world view.

■ Expressing Your Unique World View ■

What do I mean when I talk about a world view? By this I mean the writer's authentic voice, or the opinions and reactions that make up the unique viewpoint on life. "Roseanne" blasted onto the entertainment scenes with her distinctive view of the homemaker as "Domestic Goddess," while Tim Allen's "Home Improvement" is centered on a very humorous yet honest examination of being a male at this time in history. In fact, most people whose success explodes upon the world stage become popular specifically because of their unique world view. You can see it in screenwriters such as Quentin Tarantino and Christopher McQuarry, filmmakers like the Coen brothers or Albert

Brooks, actors like Jim Carrey, or broadcasting personalities such as Rosie O'Donnell and RuPaul. Unlike the cookie-cutter sameness provided by formulas, it is this distinctiveness that make these people stars, and their originality comes from their willingness to find inventive ways of expressing their personal truths.

The more you make contact with your own personal insights and passions, the more vivid and original your writing will be. For example, let's say you're writing about a mother who is very frightening to her child. Through your right-brain creativity, you remember a powerful image from your childhood of your mother wearing bright red shoes. Because that image immediately evokes in you exactly the kind of emotions you want your audience to have, you might decide to include that scene exactly as you remember it.

However, the audience wasn't raised by your mother, so chances are that the image of red shoes will not provoke in them the same kinds of feelings you have. That's why you use craft—to make sure that the audience can translate your personal insights into more universal terms. In this case, you might add dialogue, describe appropriate mood music, or do whatever you think is necessary to make the image's significance clear.

The awareness that you must help the audience make the desired associations is the beginning of the respect for the unique contribution of craft. The recognition that you need original, imaginative, and inventive impulses to translate those associations is the beginning of appreciation for true creativity. After reading thousands of scripts, I can tell you that the best scripts are those in which both craft and creativity are working at the highest possible level.

■ Asking the Right Questions ■

In searching for your own writing approach, it can be helpful to remember that in many ways, the creative process is really just a question and answer process. You can focus on craft to trigger the "function" questions in your mind, then search through your creative instincts to find answers. Once you have your own unique way of creating a bridge between these "left brain/ right brain" functions, you can then go back and forth until you find an answer that feels intuitively right, yet still addresses any craft needs your story may have.

Having access to both aspects of the creative process allows you to set up a "bridge" between the left and right sides of your mind. You can then move back and forth whenever you need new insight or inspiration. That shuttle process is the central active energy of the creative experience. Its allows your mind to scan from side to side to seek out your best solutions.

The problem with formulaic approaches is that they tell you to go about writing in the opposite way. By telling you what the answers must be, formulas force your creative "question and answer" process to focus only on very limited questions that produce predetermined results. Almost like the game show "Jeopardy," by determining what questions you ask, formulas control your entire creative process. That may feel helpful at first because it minimizes initial confusion, but once you lose control of your creative questions, you have also lost control of your story and your script.

Many writers are scared to let go of formulas and trust their instincts. Yet it has been my experience that people who care enough to devote time, money, and energy to mastering the creative process usually have a very strong and very accurate internal guidance system. Their problem is that they don't listen to it! For example, when I give notes on a script, the writers are already aware of the problems we're discussing. They had sensed the problems beforehand, but didn't listen to their instincts because those impulses were contrary to existing formulas or because they didn't understand what their creative discomfort meant.

When the creative process is not recognized as the basic "question and answer" process it is, writers can become panicked because they associate its search mode with being lost and losing control. However, the real problem is not that their minds are searching for answers, but that they are not recognizing the right answers if and when they find them.

Honor Your Impulses

One of your main goals as a writer is to find a process that gives you access to both the inventiveness of creativity and the clarity of craft, while still feeling genuinely authentic and comfortable. That means you must learn to recognize and respect those inner signals—both the "click" that happens when something feels right, and the nudging discomfort when something is wrong. Without that, you won't be able to "hear" the audience's needs and hungers. But most importantly, without it, you will never experience the deepest and most fulfilling satisfaction of being a writer.

Every time you tell yourself, "If I were a really good writer, I wouldn't have this problem," you stop your creative juices from flowing. What you need to do instead is learn to accept your instincts as a constant and important part of the creative process. Those impulses need to be "translated" through craft, but it's your inner truths and unique world view that are invaluable in becoming the writer you want to be.

The more you listen to your instincts, the more freely your creativity will function. That's why honoring your impulses is an indispensable step in becoming the best possible writer you can be. Yet even the best intuitive gut in the world is no good unless you can understand its messages.

That's why your goal should be to develop an *educated gut,* which is where the intellectual and emotional meet. When you have an "educated gut," it means that you receive visceral signals from your creative instincts, yet have enough command of craft to translate their message with clarity and confidence. Once you have an educated gut, you will feel freer to explore the outer reaches of both craft and creativity. You can be confident that you will find your way home again, even though you are momentarily lost. That's when writing becomes really fun, because you are able to make up your own rules and techniques, ones that are truest to the unique challenges of your individual project.

Accessing your own internal signals is also the best way of discovering your unique world view, as well as giving you insight about how to convey it to others.

■ Easy Doesn't Mean Good ■

Never think there is a direct correlation between how easy it is for you to get your story on paper and how good a writer you are. Just because it's hard for you doesn't mean that you aren't talented, and just because it comes easily doesn't mean that you are good. I know tremendously talented writers who agonize over every word and take months to finish a screenplay. I also know writers who can knock off a script in a weekend but who do very ordinary work.

The only thing that determines whether you are a good writer is what's on the page at the end of the process. The rest of it—the long nights of creative angst, the indecision, the confusion—are just your creative "modus operandi." You may or may not be able to change your creative process, but it doesn't usually matter to the outside world (except maybe friends and family) as long as you ultimately produce a strong script.

Another reason not to get too frustrated if some aspect of screenwriting is hard is because most writers have difficulty with at least one aspect no matter how easily the rest of it comes. The only thing you need to do is be honest with yourself, and know your strengths and weaknesses so that you can take them into account when you are scheduling a deadline. Beyond that, it is more important to focus on learning to identify and trust your process. Once you finally get the career break you dream of, when the pressure is on and you're out of your comfort zone, then one of the few things that can give you a sense of confidence is already knowing what your "modus operandi" is, and how to use that to your advantage to meet the challenges of the situation.

■ Don't Hurry Past the Discomfort ■

Another reason writers turn to formulas rather than develop their own unique talent is that they simply aren't willing to tolerate the emotional and intellectual discomfort that often accompanies the creative process.

It's very tempting to skip whatever aspects of the writing process are hard for them. Instead of staying with the discomfort until they find a solution that really feels right, writers often deny themselves that satisfaction because they can't stand the sense of uncertainty. Ironically, charging past the real complexities of the creative process too quickly forces writers to forgo the sense of clarity for which they hunger. In the effort to have a sense of security, they pass up the chance to obtain true success.

The truth is that no writer can get through the screenplay process without moments of doubt, confusion, or discomfort. Thinking that "If I were really talented, this wouldn't be hard," can not only be potentially crippling, but it's not true.

So instead of worrying that some aspect of writing is hard for you, work on your own tolerance for discomfort. Try different approaches. Experiment. Keep what works, and toss out what doesn't. There is no right way to write, only a way that works for you. Talented painters know they have a much better chance of success once they discover whether they prefer to work with charcoal or oils, at morning or night, doing portraiture or landscapes.

Similarly, you need to spend the time and the effort to find what works for you. That may mean discovering the writing styles, topics, times of day, writing implements, and even locations that make it easier for you to concentrate and focus on your scripts. Taking classes, reading books like this, or comparing notes with other writers can jog your creative energies, but always remember that nothing is more important than being in touch with your own creative instincts and developing an approach that works for you.

QUESTIONS

1. Have you used screenwriting formulas before?
   How did they work for you?
   Did they make you feel safe and comfortable?
   Did they make you feel confined and trapped?
   Were you pleased with the end result?
   Were you comfortable with the process?

2. Which aspect is easier for you—craft or creativity?

3. Which is a stronger drive for you—self-expression or fear of exposure?

4. How much do you trust yourself as a writer?

5. What do you think your weaknesses are?

   What are your strengths?

6. Which phase of the writing process comes easiest to you?
   The beginning? The middle? The end?

7. Which part makes you most nervous?
   Why?

8. Next time you write a screenplay, do you have any thoughts about what you'd like to do differently?

9. How often do you second-guess your own instincts?

10. When you get back comments on your own writing, how often do they address the same concerns you already had?

11. Can you tell when you've found a solution that feels right?

12. What do your own gut sensations feel like?
    How easy is it for you to translate these sensations?

The Most Valuable Tool You Have

Now that you understand both the audience's needs and your own internal process, how do you select an idea that is rich enough to satisfy both?

I believe that if there is something about an idea that genuinely excites you, there is a way to tell that story so that others can feel the same excitement. But in order to do that, you need to find out *exactly* what it is about the idea that excites you. What is it about the idea that captures your imagination? What makes it seem important to you? Why do you want to tell that story?

The Dramatic Center

The greatest tool that you as a writer have is that visceral "click," that sudden jolt, that spasm of excitement that spontaneously occurs when you hear something that excites your subconscious. That sensation can make you jump up in the middle of the night and grab a pencil, "sssh" everyone so that you can hear the rest of a news item on TV, or rip out a magazine article in your doctor's waiting room. Of all the creative impulses that a writer can feel, this one is the most important, because it signals the moment when an idea with real personal power has suddenly bubbled up from your subconscious. That's when the usually hidden message is most accessible to your conscious mind.

I call that unique combination of creative inspiration and physical sensation the *dramatic center*. It marks the exact epicenter of your emotional excitement about an idea. The dramatic center is supremely valuable for several reasons. It clarifies just what it is about the idea that seems so important to you. It also allows you to know what emotions you want to elicit in your viewers. You want the audience to have an experience that leads them to feel the way you do about your story.

Another reason it's so valuable is that many writers find it difficult to penetrate or reveal their deepest emotional concerns. An idea that has a powerful hold on the individual can sometimes be hard for a writer to gain access to through rational thinking because of subconscious resistance. But at that exact moment of eruption, the very power that makes an idea explode up to your conscious level signals the presence of a deeply held personal truth.

The moment of discovery is usually accompanied by a visceral sensation. For me it's a sudden intake of breath and a tightening at the top of my back; for you, it might be a rush of adrenaline or a clutching feeling in your chest. No matter what its form, its usefulness comes from the fact that its unmistakable physical signal means you can always locate it in your body. That allows you to return to the core of your inspiration whenever you begin to feel lost. The physical sensation that accompanies a dramatic center can function almost like the beep-beep-beep of a Geiger counter, guiding you back to that core whenever you feel you may be drifting away. As a result, you will have a compass that can be your infallible guide through all the difficult hours of soul-searching and decision making it takes to write a good script.

To illustrate the power of the dramatic center, let's say you were hired to write an updated version of *Othello*. At first glance, it's easy to see that the play's theme is jealousy, and you could always start generating your approach to the material from that kind of intellectual observation. But I guarantee that your script will be much more explosive once you are really in touch with what jealousy means to you. How do you feel about feeling jealous? Proud? Ashamed? Possessive? Exhilarated? What exactly makes you jealous and why? Suddenly you are drawing from a much richer, more stimulating pool of images and associations, one that allows the audience to glimpse the world through your eyes—giving them the taste of new information, which is what makes a story so exciting.

Look what Peter Shaffer did when he was writing *Amadeus*. It would have been easy to write a straightforward, chronological approach to Mozart's life. Other writers might have been intrigued by Mozart's poverty, or the majesty of the musician's creative genius. However, Shaffer was fascinated by the terror of being mediocre, and that's what he wrote about in *Amadeus*. It is his uniquely personal insight that makes his script so compelling. Not every writer has Shaffer's command of craft. But writers will always deliver their best material when they are working from a stance of passion and commitment.

A clear dramatic center helps your motivation as well. Discovering the dramatic center of an idea allows you to develop a personalized passion about the topic, which unlocks an astonishing cache of power and dedication. The more conscious you become of the power of your own personal truth, the more determined you will be to express it.

Discovering the Dramatic Center

I discovered both the existence and the power of a genuine dramatic center when I was running a small theater in Washington, D.C. I had always been intrigued by the story of Lizzie Borden, the infamous nineteenth-century woman honored in the doggerel:

> *Lizzie Borden took an ax*
> *And gave her mother forty whacks;*
> *When she saw what she had done*
> *She gave her father forty-one!*

So I announced in the fall that the last show of our spring season would be a play that I would write about Lizzie.

Now, I had always known that I was fascinated by Lizzie Borden. She was a thirty-two-year-old spinster accused of killing her father and her stepmother in 1892. She lived in a small New England town that valued propriety above all else, and Lizzie seemed to be the perfect New England spinster. She never showed her feelings in public, never criticized her family, and never spoke about her own desires. Her family was connected to one of the wealthiest families in the area, but her own father was a penny-pincher who forced the family to live in a rundown part of town, made them eat rotting mutton stew, and was generally a withdrawn and controlling man.

I spent three weeks in Fall River, Massachusetts, and by the end felt confident that I knew everything about the case. I had found a myriad of fascinating details, bits of real dialogue, and other insights that I was certain would add power and authenticity to the play.

So I began writing my script. I wrote and wrote and wrote, and threw scenes away, and wrote some more. I tried various approaches starting on the morning of the murder, beginning with the trial and doing flashbacks, and any other combination I could think of. Eventually I had written at least three drafts, which I now refer to as "rotten mutton," in which I tried to cleverly arrange and rearrange the details of the real chronological story. Unfortunately, each version was worse than the one before.

Meanwhile, the clock was ticking. I had publicly committed my theater to a play on Lizzie Borden, and the more lost I got, the more desperate I got. I had to find out what was wrong with my script!

Then one night I was pacing the floor trying to figure out what to try next. I started asking myself again and again why I had wanted to write the play in the first place, and suddenly realized that I identified with Lizzie Borden! I didn't consciously understand why, but I immediately recognized the truth of the visceral thunderbolt. As I kept exploring, my entire body began to feel constricted, and eventually I realized that, for me, Lizzie was a symbol of repression. Although I had been born a hundred years later and raised in a seemingly different world, I saw in her story the same anger and frustration that I had felt trying (unsuccessfully) to be a proper Southern belle.

Once I understood that repression was the dramatic center of my story, I understood why all of the "rotten mutton" drafts had been so ineffective. I had been making creative choices almost at random, blindly following conventional formats simply because I didn't know what I was trying to say. Once I understood that the play was about repression, everything suddenly became clear.

My first realization was that my story roller coaster had to be designed in such a way that the audience would experience the same relentless sense of constriction and confinement that I felt was crucial to understanding Lizzie. My earlier dramatizations of Lizzie had focused on various grisly aspects of her personal life, thus creating a jagged roller coaster such as this pattern:

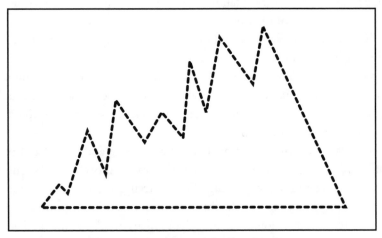

Figure 4-1   Jagged Roller Coaster

However, now that I knew I didn't want the audience to have an opportunity for venting their sense of frustration, I knew I had to build the kind of roller coaster that didn't allow audience emotions to erupt. I had to create an emotional experience for them that made them as hungry for that final explosion as Lizzie was, if only to release their pent-up frustrations. My new roller coaster looked like this ever-increasing escalation of tension:

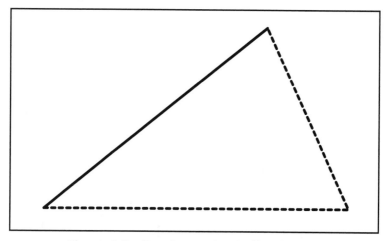

Figure 4-2   Ever-increasing Roller Coaster

Once I had a clear sense of the structure I was trying to build, the next level of decision making concerned the plot and characters. Eventually I changed the piece from a portrayal of Lizzie's actual life into a broader piece. Now Lizzie was only one of four period women suffering terribly from deep internal trauma but not allowed to express themselves because of societal expectation. At the beginning of the play they seemed like characters from *Little Women*. By the end, the audience realized that three of the women were well mannered but completely insane. One woman had never accepted the death of her fiancé years ago, one had never gotten over the sudden loss of a child, and one pretended to love her sickly elder sister, while actually letting the woman starve to death during the course of the play. Only Lizzie refused to ignore her own emotions, and only Lizzie had any chance of breaking out of her confines. Unfortunately, with no healthy role models for conflict resolution, her solution was ghastly, but when the play ended (just before the murders) the audience almost cheered! Not because they approved of her morality, but because they had developed their own deep need to vent the sense of confinement and restriction they had experienced during the course of the play.

Clarity on my dramatic center also helped me understand exactly what questions I wanted the audience to be thinking about as they watched the play. It helped me understand how to use stylistic elements to enhance the audience's sense of confinement and restriction. It showed me how to use dialogue to intensify the characters' sense of isolation, how to use colors to express the monotony of such a limited way of life, how to choose textures which would best convey the rigidity of that world, and even what kind of music I wanted to use. I'm not saying that every audience member consciously understood that the play was about repression. However, the version I finally staged was quite successful, because once I knew the epicenter of the idea, I had both the inspiration and the clarity to make exciting and unified choices throughout the play. That allowed me to send the same unified message to the audience on both the conscious and subconscious levels.

That's why I'm such a big believer in the dramatic center. It provides you with a crystal-clear understanding of the unifying dynamic of your story, allowing all the components to merge into one cohesive whole. Unfortunately, most writers don't feel the need to be so specific about what intrigues them about an idea. They often assume that if they feel drawn to a topic, the reasons are self-evident, or contained within the external elements of the idea. However, the real creative power of your topic lies not in external packaging, but in your internal associations with the idea. Often it's not the events, but the interpretation that is riveting. When writers begin to use story material as a Rorschach test to reflect the issues that are important to them, suddenly the same basic topic begins to come to life.

Dramatic Center vs. Theme

When I talk about the dramatic center in my classes, I am often asked about the difference between the dramatic center and the theme. From the point of view of the audience, the two terms may seem very much the same. In fact, if you asked audience members to express what emotional message they got from your story, their attempts to articulate their emotional realization might sound very much like a theme.

However, a dramatic center is a visceral sensation that is an internal tool for the writer. One definition would be to say that it is how you, the writer, *feel* about the theme. As experienced from the point of view of the writer, theme is analytical and objective, while a dramatic center is emotional and subjective. Theme is a conscious statement of intent, an intellectualized observation of impersonal assumptions, while a dramatic center is an impassioned insight into your personal values. The advantage of using a theme as the focus of your creative efforts is that it's often easier to access, since it is both external and conscious. But an intellectualized idea doesn't give out the clear beep-beep-beep of an internal Geiger counter. It simply doesn't have the same emotional power.

Finding that internal Geiger counter is so valuable because once you've found it, its visceral signals can be located again no matter how tired or discouraged or confused you get. We all know how easy it is to become lost in the writing process; one day you're confident that you're on the right track, and the next you're in the darkest despair. An idea that you are committed to only in your head can quickly become gibberish. The more you think, the more you second-guess yourself, and soon you're reacting to reactions. Like making copies of copies, suddenly you're generations away from your original clarity and inspiration.

■ Finding Your Dramatic Center ■

Each idea you have contains its own dramatic center, but in order to have access to its full power, you must locate and identify it exactly.

The way it usually happens for me is that I'll be reading an article or some other research material when suddenly I'll feel that jolt that I've come to know and value so well. I immediately stop what I'm doing and give all of my attention to memorizing the physical sensation while it's still fresh in my body. I then try to find a word, an image, or a sound that I can use as a reminder to help me find it again whenever I need to regain clarity. Then I test it, to make sure that the image or phrase provokes the same reaction each time I think about it. With Lizzie, I eventually found a piece of music that did the trick; with a screenplay I was going to direct, it was a mental photograph. Every time I summoned it into my consciousness, I felt the same thunderbolt of compassion that was my dramatic center for that project.

One of the ways I know I've found the real dramatic center of my idea is that I feel a visceral click, a compelling mix of relief, clarity, certainty, and excitement. Another way is that my mind begins to act like a magnet for images, music, and ideas that I may not have thought about for years. Suddenly

I remember a painting I used to love, or a piece of music that once touched me deeply. The old saw, "Nothing is wasted on a writer," suddenly seems amazingly true. Within minutes, concepts and images that may have been floating around in my mind suddenly make sense, and I can see how the dramatic center expresses the connection between them.

The important thing to remember is that you're not looking for an intellectualized idea, but a sensation, a jolt of excitement that is strong enough to be recognized whenever you need to find it again. It's also important to make sure that you write it down, or find some other way to remind yourself exactly how the sensation felt, and what triggered it. You may think you'll remember it, but you won't. The very fact that it's a momentary breakthrough from your subconscious almost guarantees that your defense mechanisms will swallow it up again as soon as they get a chance. So make sure that you've jotted down the idea or image, so that you can come back to it later and find it again.

Ideally, you should try to identify your dramatic center before you ever write a line, but often that's not possible. It's good to start looking for it as soon as possible; it's often easier to locate before you become locked into preconceptions regarding your material. Even when it's not coming easily, you should never give up. If you wonder whether you've found it or not, then you probably haven't, because the sense of confidence and clarity you instinctively feel once you've found your "compass" is unmistakable.

Sometimes the dramatic center comes first, and as you explore the sensation, you discover what your story should be. Sometimes it happens the other way around. You've discovered an idea you'd love to write about but can't figure out exactly what the dramatic center is. If you are able to find your compass early, it will help you ensure that the many layers of your story all express the same world view. No matter how long it takes, you should never submit a screenplay until you are certain that you have found your dramatic center and incorporated the resulting creative discoveries into your script.

One way to encourage the emergence of the dramatic center of an idea that intrigues you is simply to be honest. Hemingway once said, "Write the truest sentence you know," and I think that's particularly true for finding the dramatic center of your idea. The dramatic center is such a deep expression of who you are and what you believe, that anything less than your deepest truth is unlikely to reveal it. For a writer, a story is the way to tell the truth. You must believe in what your story says, which means that you have to get deep-down honest. In that sense, *every* story is a personal confession.

That is not to say that all writing should be autobiographical. Many writers become blocked when they try to create a literal recreation of their own lives. They have not yet become aware of why a certain incident is so important to them, so they can't present it to others with clarity. Even when you're writing something that seems to be entirely fictional, if the idea really "calls" to you, there is something in the idea that really touches your core.

The advice "write what you know" may help you to discover your dramatic center, but it also can be misleading. Many people think that it means you must write about only the events that have actually happened to you. "What you know" can also include those topics that you are really drawn to, those topics that set your imagination swirling, whether or not you have actually experienced them. Even if your goal is to write the world's greatest genre piece, you need to find some way to transcend the audience's expectations. You can't do that without gaining access to your own imagination, creativity, and insights as to why this genre calls to you. These insights, which arise during your soul-searching, are what make writing exciting. My friend, writer Oliver Hailey, used to say that he loved to write because he loved to find out what he thought about things!

Another way to discover the dramatic center of your idea is to develop a profile of yourself as an artist. Ask yourself what type of stories historically have caught your attention. Are there places or times in the past that you feel passionate about? Are current social issues or personalities intriguing to you? The reason this process can be helpful is that since your dramatic center is a statement of personal truths, there are often similarities between the dramatic centers of various pieces. Therefore, once you are able to locate the dramatic center in any of your works or ideas, it may be a good clue to finding it in your current piece.

It can also be helpful to go through your research, or to read related items, to see if any phrase, picture, or image suddenly sparks your interest. Sometimes, when writers become stuck at the research stage, they're instinctively looking for the dramatic center, that key that can unlock their inspiration.

Yet for all its power and importance, your dramatic center is only one criterion for how you should select ideas to write about. In the next chapter, we'll discuss the other crucial element you must consider before you commit to a story idea.

In trying to determine what the dramatic center of your story is, here are some questions you can ask yourself:

1. Did you feel a physical sensation of excitement when you first came upon the idea?

2. If you concentrate on the idea and the associations that come with it, do you always feel that same sensation?
   The same excitement?

3. Do you still believe in it as much as you did at the beginning?
   Do you really believe what your story is saying?

4. Do you feel that the world needs to hear what your story has to say?
   Why?

5. What new insight do you have into the topic?

6. Do you wish this insight had been expressed before?

7. If you had "discovered" these insights sooner, how would they have changed your life?

8. What fascinates you most about the story?
   Is it the characters' behavior?
   Their attitudes?
   Their problems?
   Their situation?
   Their skills?
   How they solve the problem?
   Why they are facing the problem?
   How they are reacting to the problem?

9. What is the emotional truth of your story?

10. Why do you think you're the right person to write this story?
    Does this material remind you of an issue or conflict in your life?

11. What do you think is the most compelling aspect of the story?
    Why are you writing this particular "take" on the story, and not other options?

12. What new understanding do you want your audience to gain?

13. How do you want your audience to feel about this story?

14. How do you want your audience to feel during this story?

15. How do you feel about spending six months or a year on this topic?

16. Do you really want to write this idea or is it one you think you should write?

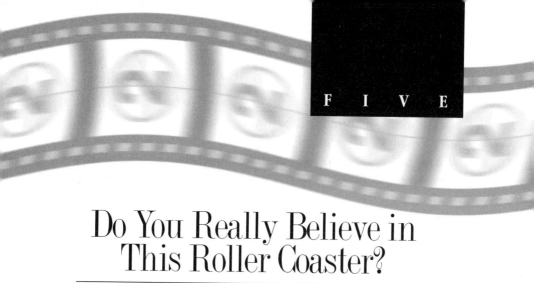

Do You Really Believe in This Roller Coaster?

Let's say you have an idea that appeals to you. The next step is to decide if you're really committed to building that roller coaster at this time in your career. This decision involves knowing where you want to go with your screenwriting, and also whether you truly think writing this screenplay will bring you closer to your goal. It's a crucial decision, because the central idea behind your story is probably the single most important element in determining how it will fare in the marketplace.

Yet the more I work with emerging screenwriters, the more I realize that they are making these crucial decisions based on limited, dated, and even inaccurate perceptions of the industry. Most writers have only the vaguest sense of what the commercial realities are, and they make crucial decisions on inaccurate or incomplete information.

Some of the "homework" you need to do in order to make realistic decisions here is external. Do you know the difference in lifestyle, pace, work process, and income between writing features, TV movies, prime time series, or daytime dramas? Do you understand the different kinds of budgets (and therefore the different kinds of production values) possible in mainstream studio films and independent productions?

The most important questions you must ask—and be determined to answer—are: "Can I really commit to this idea?" "Will this script position me as the kind of writer I want to become?" "Will this idea appeal to the kind of audience I want to attract?" Honestly exploring these issues can be a little unsettling for many writers, so they are eager to hurry past this stage of the creative process. I suggest, however, that you do emotional homework to be certain that you are comfortable with your decision.

How much you believe in the idea, how confident you are that you can bring it to life, and how proud you expect to feel about the final outcome will all have an impact on every aspect of your writing. In fact, your level of commitment to the idea is often the key factor in determining whether you ever complete your screenplay. Even after your script is written, your commitment will continue to influence its chances of success because selling a script is hard work, and most writers eventually give up unless they are genuinely excited about and proud of their screenplay.

In this chapter, we're going to examine some of the Hollywood myths, explain some fundamental industry realities, and help you understand how to assess your story's potential in the commercial market.

What is Commercial?

Many emerging screenwriters use the word "commercial" to describe any film or television script that gets made. They study all different kinds of films and television programs, and lump them all together under the category "commercial." They then look for common denominators between these cinematic stories, searching for patterns, lists of ingredients, or whatever else they can find to "copy" in order to have their own commercial success.

The problem with this process is that writers often clump together categories or forms that appeal to completely different audiences, demographics, and entertainment needs. So rather than finding a common denominator that is practical, useful, and accurate, their search for the secrets to commercial success usually ends with observations which are vague, confusing, or totally wrong for the kind of story roller coaster they intend to create. Ideas deemed "commercial" are the ones in which some buyer in the marketplace feels confident that audiences will be eager to ride; "uncommercial" means that the same party has decided a ticket to that roller coaster would be too hard to sell.

Another connotation of commercial is the industry term *high concept*, which means that the skeletal idea is enough to indicate to viewers what kind of emotional experience the movie will provide without needing to know small details. For example, the moment potential viewers heard about *Twister,* it was easy for them to imagine what kinds of thrills and excitement that movie was likely to provide.

■ Commercial = Box Office Trends? ■

Another approach that's often used to define what's commercial is to watch what's currently doing well at the box office or in the TV ratings. A similar mistake that a lot of writers make is to think it's a safe bet to start cranking out some new version of whatever's hot. That's one of the biggest mistakes you can make, because by the time you finish your screenplay, the industry will already be so flooded with similar stories that your idea will not only seem dated but perhaps even cliché.

The entertainment marketplace, just like the financial marketplace, is driven by supply and demand. An idea that's excitingly original when it first appears quickly loses its appeal once it becomes familiar. The same "here today, gone tomorrow" quality is true of almost any other trendy element of a screenplay, and if you think about it for a moment, you'll understand why. In Chapter Two we talked about how audiences are hungry for new sensations. The neophile passion is insatiable. Viewers are always on a quest for new information. The trouble is that novelty can last only so long before viewers get bored and start longing for something else.

You can see this in statistics that show more than half of the biggest box office hits are done in genres that were not popular when the movie arrived on the scene, and the same is true of successful television series as well. In fact, if you're going to use the current box office/TV ratings as any kind of gauge in deciding what to write, you should look for the genres that *aren't* currently being done, because the marketplace pendulum always swings.

■ Commercial = Hot Topics? ■

The same hunger for the new that affects a genre's appeal also affects the audience's interest in provocative topics. How society feels at any given time about a controversial social issue, for instance, can have a profound impact on your script's commercial potential. Obviously you can't always predict exactly how attitudes will change in the future, but there are somewhat recognizable cycles that you can train yourself to notice. Most issues move through our society like waves, and a script's commercial potential will be powerfully affected by when it appears in this cycle.

The fastest cycle is that of a *social fad,* which is why cinematic roller coasters that are based on fads are a bad bet. For example, right now "angel" movies may seem hot after the success of *Michael, The Preacher's Wife,* and TV shows like "Touched by an Angel." Additionally, features like *Lambada* can take so long to develop that the fad's popularity is gone before the movie is even released.

The cycle of a *social issue* lasts longer. Early in the cycle, when the level of public knowledge or comfort level is low, a script dealing with that topic will often get rejected for being too controversial. The same script can suddenly seem highly commercial if it hits the marketplace just as the subject is coming to national consciousness. However, societal attitudes adjust quickly, and once the wave crests, the audience grows bored with that topic unless your script offers a new viewpoint or twist.

Some recent examples were the rise and fall of "trash talk shows," or "women in jeopardy" TV movies of the week. Years ago, *Kramer vs. Kramer* or *Unmarried Woman* offered a serious exploration into the idea of families adjusting to divorce. Eventually such issues become more commonplace, and at that point, you began to see comic treatments such as *Mrs. Doubtfire.*

The most lasting changes are in *social direction*, which reflect fundamental shifts in public sensibilities. *Thelma and Louise* got a lot of its emotional power from the novelty of two strong women in an action buddy film. Some early "clone" films such as *The Quick and the Dead*, which tried to duplicate the "woman as action hero" idea, were not successful in the box office, but now there's a growing acceptance of women starring in more exciting, mainstream films, such as *The Net.* You can see this on the network's prime time schedules as well.

■ Commercial = The "More!" Mentality? ■

Because it's so difficult to predict what's going to be the next big trend, the entertainment industry has developed other ways to ensure exciting sensations for viewers by finding technologies and provocative visual elements that promise to give the audience *more!* "Moreness" can occur in the areas of action, special effects, sound technologies, visual techniques, sexuality, or any other aspect that offers potential intensity. Yet even "More!" has only temporary appeal because its uniqueness is only a matter of degrees.

For example, *Terminator 2, Jurassic Park,* Eddy Murphy's *The Nutty Professor, Who Framed Roger Rabbit, Terminal Velocity,* and *Toy Story* were on the cutting edge of technology, and took countless dollars and man-hours to achieve. Each movie was dazzling and unique at the time, but now, as soon as viewers have seen it, they want more!

The basis of the entire *more!* mentality is the desire to create a sense of "event" that gets viewers "out of their heads" and completely absorbed in the world of the story. But does it usually work? How many films or television shows have you really enjoyed to such an extent? How many times have you felt that ideal sensation of being totally involved?

Probably not very often. That's because hot spots of sensation are not emotionally satisfying unless they are strung together in such a way that they develop a meaningful "big picture" for viewers.

So don't look at the external ingredients of successful films and TV shows; look at the roller-coaster experience they provide instead. Audiences go to films to experience sensations, visceral thrills, and emotional revelations, so any story that will provoke strong emotions in viewers has a better chance of being produced.

For example, look at some of the top-grossing films of all time:

STAR WARS	THE EXORCIST
E.T.	THE STING
JAWS	THE EMPIRE STRIKES BACK
THE SOUND OF MUSIC	BATMAN
THE GODFATHER	JURASSIC PARK
GONE WITH THE WIND	INDEPENDENCE DAY

Here's a short list of some of the most successful television shows, as well:

I LOVE LUCY	MARY TYLER MOORE
ER	ST. ELSEWHERE
ORIGINAL COSBY SHOW	M.A.S.H
ROSEANNE	ALL IN THE FAMILY

See? The only thing these hits have in common is the ability to provoke strong emotions in viewers.

The bad news is that there are no absolutes when it comes to the tangible ingredients of what's commercial. But the good news is that once you accept that essential truth, you can stop worrying about trying to be commercial and learn to develop other criteria for deciding whether or not you want to pursue a screenplay idea.

I can hear you gasping now, but before you panic, think about what I'm saying. I am not recommending that you ignore the realities of the marketplace. Playing ostrich about the financial considerations in an industry that lives and dies by box office numbers and TV ratings is a sure-fire prescription for frustration and disappointment, but so is searching for a magical formula or list of ingredients that simply doesn't exist.

So rather than worrying about whether your idea is commercial, you should be focusing on whether your idea can really provoke strong, exciting, satisfying emotions for viewers. Ultimately what really matters is the quality of the roller-coaster ride. To be a genuine hit, it's not enough that a TV show get a good sampling of curious viewers when it first comes on the air, or for a film to attract viewers during its first weekend in release. To stay in the marketplace long enough to make money, a cinematic story must satisfy viewers so that they will come back again or recommend it to their friends. In order to do that, it must provide a fulfilling story experience.

The more your story appeals to the four basic hungers we discussed in Chapter Two (new information, emotional bonding, conflict resolution, and the promise of completion), the better your chances are of someone in the industry sensing that your screenplay would be the blueprint for a great roller coaster.

■ The Bottom Line ■

No matter what segment of the industry appeals to you, the essential truth is that Hollywood wants money. Ideally, the industry wants every film or TV show to make millions, but at the very least it wants a reasonable return on investment. That means attracting an initial audience that finds the experience satisfying enough to recommend it to friends, thus allowing the film to stay in theaters or on TV long enough to become profitable.

Conventional wisdom claims that in order to make money, a film has to be a big studio extravaganza. Yet when you compare cost to income, the most profitable film in 1995 was *The Brothers McMullen*, which made back 50 times its cost.

■ The Concept ■

The function of your story concept is like that of the barker at a carnival. Its purpose is to attract potential riders to your roller coaster. No matter what segment of the film industry you want to write for, or what kind of TV scripts you want to create, the most important element in assessing whether it will fit the marketplace's needs is the central concept of your story.

In this context, concept means premise, basic idea, or central dilemma. The conventional wisdom is that the industry is only interested in *high concept* stories, meaning that as soon as viewers hear the basic idea, they can easily imagine what kind of roller coaster it will provide. As I already mentioned, *Twister* is high concept; the name alone conveys the wild visual excitement that story will probably create. Yet a high concept film usually has the most impact when audiences first here about it; after that, word of mouth tends to be more responsible for getting other viewers.

The main reason that high concept ideas can be such an advantage in the marketplace is that they are easy to convey. Promotion budgets are very expensive. The faster advertisers can communicate an idea to potential viewers, the less money producers will have to shell out before they can begin to make a profit. *Soft concepts*, on the other hand, are movies dependent on the personality of the people involved. In *The Evening Star* or *The Mirror has Two Faces,* for example, there is no way for viewers to anticipate what kind of emotional experience the movie will produce unless they know something about the personalities of the characters and the details of their lives.

With that kind of life-and-death outcome hanging in the balance, many writers are convinced that the only way to succeed is to write something commercial, whether or not that kind of story genuinely appeals to them. They disregard ideas for which they feel genuine passion and commit themselves instead to mainstream genre pieces; ironically, it is that very sacrifice that often prevents them from having the success they crave.

■ "So What Does Commercial Mean!?!?!?" ■

It's a question I hear all the time. In fact, more than once during the last few years a frustrated writer has stormed up to me and wailed, "Just tell me what's commercial, so I can write the stupid thing!"

Often this topic can be so frustrating because writers assume there's a tangible list of elements, such as steamy sex scenes, great action sequences, exciting car chases, happy endings, or superstar casting, that guarantee success. While it's true that many successful films have those ingredients, it's also easy to think of films like *Daylight, Ishtar,* or *Cutthroat Island* that had plenty of those elements and failed. Meanwhile, what about hits like *Babe?* It can really strain your imagination to find a list of common plot points among *Jurassic Park, The First Wives Club, Jerry Maguire, Sleepless in Seattle,* or *Toy Story.*

It's clear from studying box office winners that actual plot ingredients vary tremendously. That's because individual ingredients—no matter how good they look on paper—can only provide initial curiosity or momentary interest; they have never been, nor will be, enough to guarantee commercial success.

The reason you can't count on external ingredients to guarantee success is because what makes a film emotionally compelling is not just what happens in the positive space on the screen, but what happens in the audience's negative space as well. Some films are considered "feel good," while the wild imagery of others, such as *Close Encounters of the Third Kind,* lingers in the cultural awareness until they become icons. All of these reactions occur in the viewers' emotions, which is where hits are really made.

Understanding Commercial Issues in Films

Among professionals, the term "commercial" refers to a spectrum of factors used to gauge how well a story will fit the needs of its specific segment of the industry, which we will examine later in the chapter.

However, in its purist form, "commercial" refers to a small minority of studio films that are intentionally developed as major financial blockbuster "home runs" which compete against the other big-budget extravaganzas offered that year. The success of these commercial films is crucial; only one film in five makes a profit, so these big budget extravaganzas usually provide the bulk of the 20% success rate that keeps the studios in business.

As a result, the studios put the full weight of their financial, marketing, and cinematic techniques behind films like *Independence Day, Jurassic Park, Toy Story, 101 Dalmatians,* or even *Basic Instinct.* The stories and the production are designed to deliver as many moments of intensity as possible. As a result they are often showcased for state-of-the-art technology. The industry also considers "repeatable thrills," a term referring to films that will attract repeat (and often young) viewers, which is what drives the box office numbers through the roof.

Contrary to popular opinion, a film doesn't have to be a potential blockbuster to get made. In fact, would-be commercial hits make up only a small portion of the approximately four to five hundred Hollywood films released each year. The proportion of films made each year that consciously aim to become major would-be blockbusters is approximately one in five, at the most.

What this also means is that approximately eighty percent of films are *not commercial,* in the sense emerging screenwriters use the term. While that may sound surprising, the entire film distribution business is built on the acceptance that not every film is a potential blockbuster, nor is it intended to be. That's why there are four general distribution categories which reflect the differing budgets, casting, target audiences, marketing campaigns, and financial returns that the film industry considers realistic, based on how that segment of the movie audience has responded in the past.

The most visible, the most high-stakes, and the most financially costly segment of distribution is *main stream,* which is how films that are considered to have broad-based audience appeal are introduced to the marketplace. The most elaborate and impressive campaigns in this marketing segment are backed by multi-million dollars worth of paid TV and press advertising, such as the campaign for the first *Batman* movie. Less intense campaigns are more the norm, but even then the rule of thumb is that the cost of promoting and marketing a mainstream film will usually equal the cost of making the film.

What makes a film a candidate for a mainstream launch is usually either a major star or a hot concept, based on the assumption that one of those elements will attract a wide variety of viewers as soon as they hear about the movie. Sometimes distributors think that a mainstream audience will respond favorably to a film, but there's no element in the film that will grab immediate attention. In those cases, films are put in *limited distribution,* which means the film is shown in fewer theaters, less money is spent on the promotional campaign, and a more narrow audience is targeted. Distributors develop a launch strategy, aimed at strong *word of mouth*, the industry term for satisfied viewers who recommend the film to friends. *Sense and Sensibility* and *Fried Green Tomatoes* were launched this way. That's the only realistic chance, considering the limited budget or appeal of the topic, that can attract enough viewers to make the film a major commercial, mainstream success.

Another kind of distribution game plan is used for *specialty films.* These are films which distributors know could never be mainstream hits because of controversial topics, styles, or narrow-interest genre (like the majority of martial arts films). Movies like the newest version of *Romeo and Juliet* or *Looking for Richard* are also distributed only in specific markets, regions, or audiences, which is why it's often hard to find these films outside of major urban areas.

The last kind of segment of distribution is geared towards *art house films,* which also include most cult and foreign films. Targeted to the smallest number of potential viewers, these films are often shown in theaters that specialize in this kind of non-commercial film. *The Rocky Horror Picture Show* often plays on this theater circuit, as do the lower-profile foreign films.

What Does "Commercial" Mean in TV?

Similarly, in television "commercial" means including all of the elements that have been traditionally successful in your series or TV movie idea. Since those rules shift over time and differ according to the form of the series or TV movie idea, television shows actually have an even lower success rate than features.

Here are some general observations about factors which are used to determine a television show's commercial potential:

■ One Hour Dramas ■

The three key factors in assessing a series idea are the characters, the franchise, and the uniqueness.

The reasons *characters* are so important is that for a TV series to succeed, the audience needs to feel drawn to the characters, and want to see them week after week. There's a degree of familiarity that is needed for viewers to invite characters "into their living room," as they say in the industry, so often television stars radiate a charm, accessibility, or easy-to-relate-with quality that is less dangerous and intense than film stars.

Franchise, also an industry term, provides the characters with the authority, the right, or the expertise to be in high stakes dilemmas which can also provide a wide variety of stories. That's why you see so many series about cops, lawyers, and doctors. In contrast, when amateurs suddenly decide to run around solving murders, or a one-hour drama is set in a kindergarten school, it can strain viewers' imaginations and quickly result in a shortage of ideas for episodes.

The third element is a *distinctiveness* of concept or voice. With six networks and countless cable channels, a show can't attract an audience if it can't stand out in the crowd.

■ Sitcoms ■

Sitcoms employ the same elements, but address them in very different ways.

Characters are crucial in sitcoms because without clearly defined characters, the show's humor has to remain plot-driven instead of character-based, which is what all sitcom successes have in common.

The issue of franchise is also handled differently. Sitcoms tend to use their franchise more as an arena to generate interesting stories than as the basis of a character's legitimacy, as is seen with the news room on "Mary Tyler Moore" or the station offices on "News Radio." At least as many successful sitcoms like "Friends" or "Seinfeld" have been centered in living rooms because the franchise of a sitcom, in many ways, is the personality quirks and attitudes which "legitimize" the weekly comedic conflicts, rather than where those conflicts take place.

Distinctiveness is a key element in sitcoms which become major hits. Unique points of view, expressing "truths" the audience recognizes, but hasn't heard before—"Roseanne," "Home Improvement," "The Simpsons"—stand out in a crowded marketplace and fulfill all four core emotional needs imaginatively and unexpectedly.

■ Movies of the Week (MOW) or Miniseries ■

These made-for-television pieces, usually referred to as "longform," do not depend on such a strong emotional bonding between characters and viewers, because the audience must decide to watch these one-time events before they get to know the characters. The same "one time only" nature of these events also prevents word of mouth from being effective, except in later episodes of a miniseries.

That's why the concept is so crucial. When you're deciding whether to watch a MOW on Sunday night, all you know about that show is what you read in *TV Guide,* and perhaps what you see in an ad and/or some brief on-air promotion. Unless a provocative idea, a true-life crime sensation, some fantasy-fulfillment, high-profile casting, or the fact that the show is based on a best-selling book catches your attention, you'll probably choose to watch something else. That's why these are the elements considered commercial in this form.

What Kind of Roller Coaster Do You Want to Build?

Do you know? Are you just guessing? Are you listening to your heart, your creative instincts, or some vague list of "shoulds" about what will and will not succeed?

The best of all possible worlds, of course, is to find an idea that you would love to write about and that you are also confident has strong commercial appeal. Some writers long to create those blockbuster action/adventure megahits, but many writers simply are not drawn to such mainstream stories. They would truly be happier creating small art films, but they are afraid they will never get an agent or break into the business with anything other than a mainstream screenplay. That fear may paralyze them completely, or persuade them to ignore the cinematic stories that come from their heart. They struggle to re-create whatever conventional wisdom says the industry wants at that time. No matter how hard they work, the end result is usually uninspired because the story doesn't call to them.

If that's true of you, here are some thoughts that may help you feel less compelled to strive to create those mainstream, blockbuster films, or trite, generic TV scripts that formulas often encourage you to produce. In fact, there are many more compelling reasons why you should not.

First of all, you will only produce a great script if you have a passion for the story, and can find a genuine dramatic center in the idea that makes it come alive to you. Therefore, forcing yourself to write something that you have no real interest in is putting yourself at a tremendous disadvantage. You will be drawing your creative imagination from the most conscious, artificial, and external inspiration, such as what you've learned from studying other films. As a result, your script, compared to writers who have a genuine passion for that kind of story, will often seem forced, contrived, and lifeless.

Secondly, your numerical chances of success are much better in the non-blockbuster portions of the market. Focusing your efforts at the would-be blockbuster portion of the marketplace puts you in competition with the most established, well-paid, and well-connected screenwriters in Hollywood, many of whom do have a genuine passion for those kinds of films. You'll be up against the toughest competition in the industry. Additionally, studios have so much money riding on these films that they look for anything that might increase the movie's chance of success. Often that means selecting a screenwriter whose track record is already established rather than taking a chance on a newcomer.

Meanwhile, the producers of smaller films have just as many marketplace concerns to worry about, not the least of which is budget. You can actually weaken your chances of getting your quiet, character-driven script produced if you include a lot of extraneous car chases, crowd scenes, special effects, or other elements in an effort to be commercial, since such additions can easily make the film too expensive to produce, yet rarely have much impact on the success of the film.

Another reason is that "credits don't travel," by which I mean that if you spend time writing in one form or genre, and think that success in that area will "carry over" to the area you really want to focus on, you're in for a major disappointment. Agents, executives, producers, and directors who specialize in sitcoms, for instance, have little knowledge or interest in TV movies. The discrepancy is even more pronounced between TV and film.

The point I'm making is that there's no advantage to forcing yourself to write scripts or forms in which you have no interest, especially if you think you're doing it to advance your career. What generally happens is writers get pigeon-holed into the first area in which they succeed. It becomes surprisingly hard to cross over to other areas, so if you know where you want to go, go there.

■ Making an Informed Decision ■

First of all, make sure you do your homework. Research the marketplace and find out which companies make and distribute the kind of film you want to write. Look up the studios, networks, and producers of the kind of TV shows you want to create. There may be more of a market for your story than you originally assumed. If there is, study those films or TV shows and see if you can identify the kinds of budgets, financing, and other production considerations that they have in common.

Some good sources of information are the daily or weekly trade papers, such as *Variety* or *The Hollywood Reporter*. Even if these are hard to fully understand at first, you need to be familiar with the industry, issues, players, and "lingo" in the field you want to enter. Books like *Reel Power*, which dissects the movie industry, or books that catalogue TV shows, such as Major Canton's *Complete Reference Guide To Movies And Miniseries Made For TV*, can be immensely helpful in spotting trends and identifying companies, stars, or producers who might be interested in your scripts.

When assessing your concept, be aware that high concept stories are most important if you want to create a mainstream film. The most important consideration when committing to a concept is not whether the topic is "hot," "high concept," or "soft concept," but whether there is something about the topic that would actively attract viewers. It might be curiosity, novelty, fantasy fulfillment, or a life-affirming "feel good" experience, but the important thing is to make sure that the subject has a major component that would make viewers want to spend time in that world.

Another consideration is how well your story takes advantage of the medium. Is the jeopardy visual, or is all the emotional power in the dialogue? Are there great moments of excitement, or is the story more intellectually provocative without stirring strong emotion? Is it the kind of roller coaster whose thrills are "repeatable" (for example, such event-filled adventures as *Star Wars*), or is it a roller coaster that builds to one startling discovery (such as *The Conversation*) and then loses a lot of its impact once the audience knows the surprise?

If you think you have a great idea but are genuinely concerned that the idea isn't marketable, then don't write it now. Wait until you have more success and there is some demand for your work. Another viable alternative, if your story contains a real standout character, is to try to get your script into the hands of a major box office star who may have some interest in playing that kind of role. Studios will sometimes attempt riskier projects when major stars are attached.

Try to dig deep and be honest about your real motives for writing the particular script. Do you only want to use it as a showcase for your writing ability, or are you determined only to invest your time and effort in a script you feel confident will sell? If it's the latter case, here are some ways to work on developing an "educated gut" regarding the factors that can heighten a script's commercial appeal.

Don't fool yourself about your script's chances of success at the beginning of the process and then become bitter at the end if it gets rejected for reasons that could have been easily predicted. Another mistake I see writers make is to choose an idea they know has only limited commercial appeal, then try to force it into some commercial mold. The results of such decisions are scripts that are neither fish nor fowl; they are neither well suited to the external marketplace demands, nor do they provide the writer with the internal satisfaction of having been true to that inner voice.

■ Developing More Insight Into the Marketplace ■

1. Don't Copy the Past

Many books and classes about screenwriting use existing scripts or films as templates, but there are several reasons why that's not necessarily a good idea.

First of all, copying existing roller coasters (always placing key turning points in the same place, for example) means that you will ultimately just end up building the same roller coaster again and again. Because audiences crave new experiences, that's exactly what they don't want.

Additionally, just because a film or television show has been produced doesn't mean it's a good example of success. If you do your homework and explore the behind-the-scenes story about many a hit, you may soon discover that it was the financial deal, or star casting, or existing production commitments, or other non-script-related issues that were really the determining factor in getting a particular script produced *even though the participants knew that the screenplay itself was flawed.*

Conversely, sometimes the original script was terrific, but what you see on the screen is the result of choices and compromises that made it quite different from the script that originally got the producers excited (like that old saying about how a horse designed by a committee ends up looking like a camel). Therefore, if you blindly copy an existing roller coaster without doing your homework, you just may end up copying someone else's mistakes.

2. Study Sleepers

Studying sleepers is a good way to develop your awareness of what makes a story roller coaster successful with viewers.

Sleeper is the industry term for films that don't get a lot of promotion but manage to find their audience anyway. The reason it's better to study films that have not been the subject of one of Hollywood's major publicity campaigns is that when you try to track the emotional effectiveness of films like the first *Batman,* it's hard to separate the appeal of the actual roller-coaster experience from the carefully orchestrated "buzz."

Sleepers, however, have no such launching pad to put them in orbit. It's only the fact that viewers find them so satisfying that allows them to survive and even flourish. *Fried Green Tomatoes, The English Patient, Chariots of Fire, Home Alone,* and *The Crying Game* are movies that enjoyed this kind of success. "Seinfeld," "Cheers," and "The X-Files" were television sleepers.

3. Study Movie Previews

Next time you go to a movie, pay close attention to the coming attractions, as well as your reaction to them. Such trailers give you a chance to study the essence of a movie's concept. Notice which ones catch your interest and which ones leave you cold.

Train yourself to articulate your reasoning, so that it will rise up to your consciousness and not remain simply instinctive. Then make note of your reactions and compare them to what happens at the box office when the film is released. Were you wrong? Can you figure out why? If not, make a point of seeing the film yourself, and see if the quality of the roller coaster had anything to do with its unexpected performance at the box office.

4. Study Failure

Studying box office failures is also very important. When you hear about a film that has failed at the box office despite the fact that it seemed to have everything going for it commercially, make a point of seeing it before it disappears. That way you can discover whether its roller-coaster construction disappointed riders, whether the promotional campaign made promises the film didn't deliver, or whether the concept itself was innately flawed.

Were you right about its audience appeal? Did the concept seem limited? Does the title seem like a weird choice, like the comedy *The Housesitter,* in which the title doesn't capture the story's real center? Does the movie fail to explore the aspect of the concept which initially intrigued you? Some people felt *Striptease,* for example, was much more of a light comedy than an erotic fantasy. Was the idea interesting, but the execution flawed? Some said this about *Rob Roy,* in which the antagonist outshone the heroes.

5. Anticipate the Future

We've talked before about the social cycles that influence a topic's commercial appeal. If you are interested in writing stories dealing with such social issues, it's important to train yourself to look forward. But there are also other sensibilities which change as well, so the more you can sensitize yourself to picking up hints about attitudes, issues, and styles that will be popular in the future, the more timely any script you write can become.

Make a point of reading little-known magazines, medical journals, law journals, local newspapers, technical and scientific journals, science fiction magazines, and computer billboards for small news items. What you're looking for are stories that provide a new slant on an area of established interest, which is just about as close to a magic formula for a commercial idea as you can get.

QUESTIONS

Once you think you've found an idea which you could really be interested in, here is a list of questions to consider:

1. Do you want to write for television or film?

2. Do you know what segment of film distribution is closest to your idea?

3. Do you know what kind of TV form best fits your idea?

4. Does it fit into an identifiable portion of the market?
   Mainstream studio film or independent?
   Television series or Movie of the Week?

5. What is your goal for this script?
   To use it as a writing sample or to get it made?

6. Which studios, producers, actors, or directors have done movies with the same sensibility as yours?
   What networks, studios, writers, or producers have shown a historical interest in your kind of story?

7. Does your idea create an exciting roller coaster?
   Does it provoke strong emotions?
   Are there big emotional stakes?

8. Does it tap into universal emotions?

9. Does it tell viewers something new?
   Does it touch on an area of established curiosity?
   Does it provide a new slant?

10. Is there a reason for viewers to want to spend time in that world?
    Is it life-affirming?
    Is there an underlying idea that the viewers will want to believe?

11. Does it provide fantasy fulfillment?

12. Is there a character for viewers to bond with?

13. Is it "high concept"?

14. If it's a soft concept, is it a star vehicle?
  Will it be easy to promote?

15. Will it appeal to a wide variety of viewers?
  Why?

16. Is it in keeping with today's sensibilities?
  Is it a topic affected by current social cycles?

Structure: Designing Your Roller Coaster

Let's say that you now have an idea for a roller coaster that you really want to build. What is the next step?

Imagine that a major theme park hired you to create a new roller-coaster ride. The first thing you would do is develop an overall sense of the experience you want to create for the riders. Then you'd study the land, determine construction options, and weigh design possibilities. Eventually you'd develop a clear idea of the specific roller coaster you wanted to create. Then you would begin to select and combine roller coaster components needed to obtain the desired effect.

The same dynamic is true for developing a screenplay. Once you've committed to a story idea, it's very helpful to start thinking about what structure, what sequence of audience emotional highs and lows, would best convey your dramatic center. Once you have an overall sense of what kind of roller-coaster ride you intend to build, you will have tangible and consistent criteria for selecting the other elements of your roller coaster.

A phrase you often hear in Hollywood is "A screenplay *is* structure." That means the real power, cohesiveness, and impact of a script can be assessed by how well its overall structural pattern works. The reasons for structure's dominance is that the overall ride determines whether the audience will achieve catharsis, and whether they'll find the story emotionally satisfying or not.

Humans don't often have an opportunity to experience complete catharsis in life, which creates all the more hunger for it in stories. Yet if the audience becomes increasingly intrigued by the plot, emotionally involved with the characters, eager to know what's going to happen next, and enveloped in a unique world through clever use of style, then the components of a story roller coaster have combined to create a compelling and unified ride that carries an audience to climax and release. When both the audience's emotional and logical energies have been absorbed into the positive space of the story, then you can provide real catharsis.

One of the best examples of the primal hunger for cathartic emotional release is music. Music and dance have no words, no ideas, no plots, no facts—none of the things we consider necessary to a story. What creates the sense of structure? It is the interrelationship of elements such as sounds, rhythms, contrasts, and building intensity that can lead an audience to the state of climax and release.

That's how it is with dramatic structure. Ultimately structure is not a single, isolated element, but the overall shape created by the audience's individual reactions to the elements of your story. So the sooner you begin to have a sense of which key changes are most important to your structure's shape and texture, the sooner you can begin to focus your creative energies on selecting the other story components that will help you achieve your goal.

The Power of Change

Conventional wisdom says that stories are about conflict, but as we discussed in the last chapter, the reason the aspects of change reflected in your story's structure are so crucial is that stories are really about the deeper, primal emotional dilemma centering on humans' fear of, yet need to, change. Conflict can create momentary excitement because of its theatricality, but its genuine power comes from the fact that it intensifies the likelihood of change.

Change is potent because it is the essential dynamic of life itself. It is the one common denominator that all humans face: bodies change, seasons change, lives change, relationships change, feelings change, locations change, and technologies change, so people must learn to cope with change if they want to survive. Yet as universal as change may be, people often resist it because they fear the unknown. Thus the tension between the need for change and the fear of it can be fascinating territory for stories.

Your goal as a writer is to create a specific series of emotions in your audience that lead them to *experience* your dramatic center. Every aspect of your screenplay, including the central plot, is ultimately just a means towards that end. Focusing on your intended structure can be a provocative starting point for your creative process because the roller-coaster design is really just a tangible expression of what *pattern of changes* would best convey your dramatic center to the viewers.

Choosing a Roller-Coaster Design

One way to develop clarity about structure is to ask yourself what kind of changes your story is really about, and what aspect or pattern of change most interests you. For example, one pattern that can be theatrical is a series of seemingly small changes that suddenly adds up to a huge crisis. Such films as *Quiz Show, The Firm, Bad Influence, The Scarlet Letter, The Andromeda Strain,* and *Invasion of the Body Snatchers* fit this pattern.

In contrast, sometimes the pattern of change is exciting because of its constant extremes. The TV show "ER," the horror films *Scanners, Sleuth,* and *Hellraiser* have almost continuous patterns of ups and downs. Meanwhile, *Damage, The Great Gatsby, And Now My Love,* or the classic TV series "Twilight Zone" build incrementally upward, often to one climactic moment.

Sometimes the key moment of change occurs after a crucial discovery is made, such as in *The Conversation* or *House of Games,* when many seemingly small incidents in the beginning of the story are contrasted with the major revelations occuring near the end. Some films create a series of building revelations, such as *Twelve Angry Men,* when Henry Fonda manages to change the opinions of all other eleven jurors in what seemed like an open and shut case. Others build a relentless sense of urgency and danger, such as *Jaws* or *Speed,* while others seem to start out smoothly and then become unexpectedly dangerous in the second half, such as *No Way Out.*

Key Moments of Change

Another way to focus your creative energies is to ask yourself if you can envision even the vaguest pattern of *key moments of change*. Those are the moments when the direction, speed, or texture of a roller coaster suddenly take an exciting turn, and these are often the first hints you get about your story's structure.

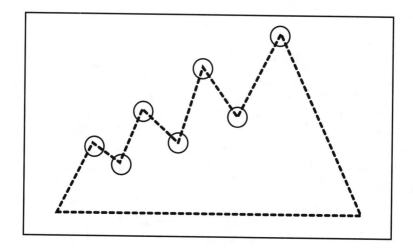

Figure 6-1   Key Moments of Change

Whatever the pattern, the more your structure can convey the sequence, pacing, and texture of these changes, the more effective your story will be, because it will communicate the same powerful dynamics to the audience on both conscious and subconscious levels. For example, in *The Day of the Jackal,* the dramatic center of the idea had to do with the ever-present tension of the professional assassin. He was on a relentless mission, and there was no real emotional release for him until the mission was done. Making sure the audience felt the sensation of building tension was crucial to the story. The plot contained several murders, but the roller coaster intentionally minimized the impact of individual scenes in order to maintain an overall taut, tense upward build. Thus what could have been a roller coaster that looked like this:

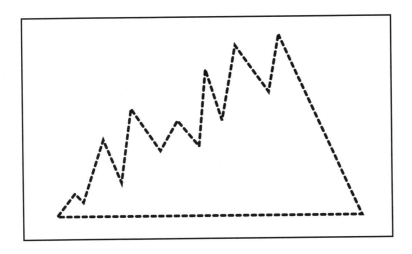

Figure 6-2   Jagged Roller Coaster

ended up looking like this:

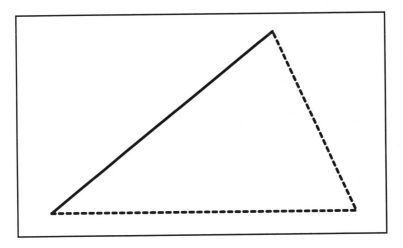

Figure 6-3   Generic Roller Coaster

thus forcing the audience to endure the same emotional tension and hunger for the eventual resolution.

Often writers will have a visceral sense of what some of those shifts might be long before they have chosen the exact plot and character points that will eventually provoke them. For example, here's how the same story material might result in strikingly different roller coasters.

Let's say that five different writers were hired to write screenplays about the same failed marriage. One writer, who was fascinated by the slow, steady, incremental build of destructiveness and anger within the couple, would probably build a roller coaster that looks something like this:

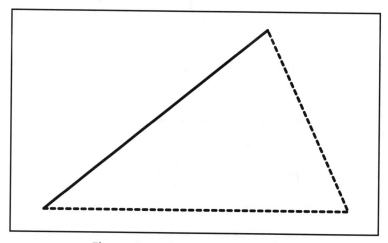

Figure 6-4   Generic Roller Coaster

The writer who was intrigued by the contrast between the couple's seemingly idyllic beginning, which suddenly and mysteriously turned vengeful one night, would probably like the audience to experience a ride more like this

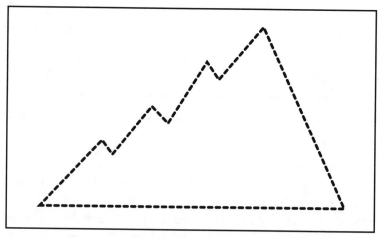

Figure 6-5   Mountain Peak Roller Coaster

The script created by the writer who was convinced that the marriage was never really happy might plant startling hints which become a larger and larger portion of the couple's life and create this kind of sensation for viewers:

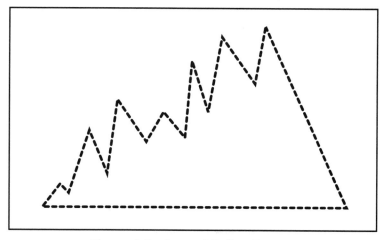

Figure 6-6   Jagged Roller Coaster

Meanwhile, the script written by the author who decided to begin the screenplay with the couple's violent, final breakup, then flash back to the beginning of the story and work forward from that point would want to create the following kind of roller-coaster experience for viewers:

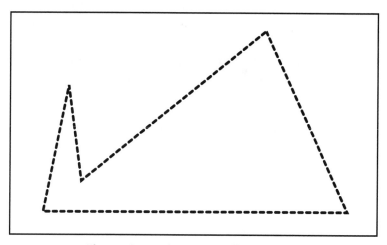

Figure 6-7   Big Bang Roller Coaster

The script written by the author who was intrigued by the image of a marriage falling apart in small moments, never big fights, might build a structure like this:

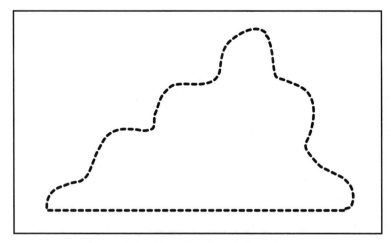

Figure 6-8   Meandering Roller Coaster

Once you truly understand structure, you can see how profoundly this creative choice affects every other aspect of writing a screenplay, which is why I disagree so strongly with formulas that tell you where you must place certain turning points, or in what order certain events must occur. By predetermining the incidents of your story, they are telling you to build the same basic roller coaster again and again. Yet the same roller coaster is exactly what viewers don't want. The audience wants new thrills, new sensations, and new information; riding the same roller coaster over and over (now how matter well designed) gets boring, because it becomes too easy for the audience to anticipate the ride.

Finding the Right Structure

As you can see, the overall structure of the story is much more dependent on the writer's own sense of excitement about the topic than the actual topic. Consequently, you must decide exactly what excites you about the topic and what sequence of emotions would best convey that excitement to the viewers.

You will find that there is a direct connection between *your* story's dramatic center, which is the specific angle of the idea that excites you, and the overall structure of the piece that you want to build for your audience. That's because it's exactly that thrill, that jolt, or that sweeping sense of ecstasy which makes the material appealing to you and therefore lets you know what sensations you want to create for your audience. Without that kind of visceral target to reach for, screenwriting can become an exercise in logic far too removed from its emotional roots to be really compelling.

Despite its importance, your dramatic center is only one sensation, one moment of emotional revelation. Yet humans don't experience emotions in isolation, but in context or juxtaposition with other emotional states. Getting viewers into your climactic emotional state involves creating a series of emotional transitions that lead them to that crucial moment. Therefore, once you know what emotional state you want your audience to ultimately achieve, you can develop clarity about what preceding emotional reactions you will need to provoke for viewers to experience your dramatic center.

Some of the most intense moments in life are those moments of change when people shift in their attitudes or assessments from one state of mind to another. For example, betrayal is a painful emotional state, and can therefore be quite dramatic. However, the actual moment of betrayal is only the end result of a series of previous feelings and events, such as the pleasure of getting to know someone new, developing a friendship with that person, thinking that the person is trustworthy, taking a big chance with that person, and then finding yourself betrayed. The more confident people are of their assessment of the situation, the more powerful the shift can be. In fact, the moment of betrayal becomes even more powerful because of the contrast with the previous moments of trust and sharing.

The same is true with stories. It is actually the shift in emotional states, the progression of feelings, that makes a story dynamic, and so, as soon as possible you need to understand exactly what emotional transitions are necessary to convey the core dynamics of your story. It's important to remember that you want your viewers to experience your world view, rather than just observe it passively or think about it later. Making sure that you create the kind of "felt experience" of inner shifts that best conveys your dramatic center to your audience is the primary goal of a screenwriter.

The pattern of how the audience experiences those shifts and changes determines the structure of your story. The process of realizing what your story's structure should be can be influenced by your internal creative process, your writing habits, or even your story idea. Sometimes you have clarity about your structure as soon as you feel drawn to an idea, and sometimes your understanding evolves slowly. So don't be concerned if it takes you a while to recognize exactly what kind of roller-coaster ride you want to create. What matters is that when you're writing final drafts, you have both clarity and confidence about the choice you've made, allowing you to combine your creativity and craft to ensure its success.

In the next chapter, let's discuss the role of the plot in creating your story roller coaster.

Q U E S T I O N S

Here are some questions to help focus your creative energies:

1. Do you have a clear sense of the overall shape of the roller coaster you are trying to design?

2. What is the dramatic center of your story?

3. What pattern of change intrigues you?

4. Do you have a clear sense of the overall shape of roller coaster that would best convey those sensations?

5. What do you want your audience to feel?

6. What textures would best convey that emotional quality?
    Smooth? Jagged? Abrupt? Slow? Fast?

7. What previous emotional states would be necessary in order to make those key moments more effective?

8. Can you think of any similar story roller coasters?

9. Did you like the sensation that roller coaster created?
    Why?

10. What is the difference between that roller coaster and the one you want to build?

11. Are there other ways you could structure your same story?
    Why do you prefer the one you've chosen?

Plot: Building Your Roller Coaster

Let's say you now have an idea what shape you want your roller coaster to be. What would happen if you simply hung the track up in the air? Obviously it wouldn't last a minute. In order for the track to function effectively, the intended design must be translated into an actual construction and supported by pillars strong enough to sustain its wild twists and turns.

The same is true for a story roller coaster. The structure is your intended design, but the plot is what actually creates the audience highs and lows by presenting story information that provokes emotion. Therefore, you want to select and arrange the story information in a way that creates, arouses, and intensifies the audience's emotional involvement until it builds to climax and release.

Writers think that a plot is just "what happens," so by the time they've chosen an idea, they already have a sense of what the events should be. Just because an image or scene occurs to you while pondering your story doesn't mean that it must be included in the screenplay. Thus it is essential that you develop clear criteria about what to include and what to eliminate as you begin to translate your concept into a plot.

The first thing is to understand the difference between plot and story. Story is all of the potential information about your idea, while plot is your selection and arrangement of pertinent information chosen to dramatize your dramatic center. For example, in my Lizzie Borden script, the story could begin at the birth of her parents and continue to Lizzie's death or even beyond. However, such a straightforward chronology of events would not provide the focus and clarity needed to bring a unique vision of the story to life. In order to separate the details of plot, you must identify the central issues, causes, obstacles, and ramifications that will express your take on the story.

How Plot Addresses the Audience's Four Needs

Your plot's primary function is to examine the process of *conflict resolution*, which involves confronting the many challenges and problems created by change. Since it is often difficult for viewers to attain clarity about the changes and conflicts in their own lives, exploring similar issues in a fictional setting can allow them to see from different perspectives, thus providing insight and understanding.

However, you also need to make sure your plot addresses the other core emotional needs of the audience. It should include enough *new information* to hold their interest, allowing them to glimpse other realities. This is what supplies much of the appeal of films like *Light the Red Lantern, Apollo 13, Phenomenon* and other stories that move viewers into worlds and sensations they may never experience on their own. Plot also must help viewers *bond* to the story. Presenting a central conflict pertinent to the viewers' lives will let an audience feel a personal connection to the story.

The last of the four emotional needs your plot must fulfill is *completion*, allowing the audience to experience the satisfaction of building to a climax, then resolution. One of the fundamental demands audiences make is that stories should "make life make sense." Therefore the ending of the story is critical to the audience's overall enjoyment. Because of the audience's hunger for closure, a plot that leaves unanswered questions won't be satisfying.

■ Moving from Inspiration to Plot ■

Many writers lose the clarity of their original vision as they struggle to create a cohesive and coherent plotline. The "big picture" fades as they try to solve a million smaller details, and the result is often a choppy, erratic screenplay that no longer addresses the aspects of the idea that first drew the writer to it. To avoid this problem, you must make conscious and consistent choices about how to use your screen time to tell the actual story you were inspired to tell. Therefore, it is crucial that you fully understand what your screenplay is really about.

In order to decide what aspect of change you want to dramatize in your screenplay, you must determine which kind of change most intrigues you and why you think that encounter with change should be told. Your plot can center on four kinds of change, all of which may appeal to viewers because they recognize such dilemmas in their own lives. *Internal change* deals with conflicts and issues inside the central character, as in *Mr. Holland's Opus.* Another kind is *interpersonal change,* in films like *Marvin's Room* or *Dolores Claiborne,* in which change is caused by interactions with other characters. *Societal change,* as in *Philadelphia* or *And The Band Played On,* deals with issues that have impact on a larger scale. *Situational change* in films like *Turbulence, Flood,* or miniseries like "Asteroid" or "Pandora's Clock," deals with external challenge.

The *inability to change* can also be dramatic. One example is the heartbreaking scene at the end of *Ordinary People* when Mary Tyler Moore's character chooses to leave rather than change her ways. In *Remains of the Day,* Anthony Hopkins's inability to change his patterns forces him and Emma Thompson to live needlessly alone, while in *Casino,* Joe Pesci's inability to accept change destroys many people's lives.

Change can be deep within a person, as in *It's a Wonderful Life,* or only in the outward circumstances, as in *National Lampoon's Christmas Vacation.* It can be a positive change, as in *Rocky,* or a tragic change, as in *Sophie's Choice.* Change can occur easily, as in *Moll Flanders,* or after great resistance, as in *Schindler's List.* Sometimes the struggle is to prevent change, as in *The Crucible,* and sometimes it is to cause change, as in *Gandhi.* Sometimes people try to ignore change, as in *Dead Ringers,* and sometimes people adapt to change, as in *The Day After.* It is always the existence or impending change that forces the plot to advance.

The reason you must see exactly what kind of change you want to explore is that your plot encompasses the information necessary to track the central change from beginning to end. Among the decisions you must make are: What is it that changes? Who faces the change? What is your view of that change? Why is it important? What are its causes? Why did it start? What makes it difficult? How is it confronted? What is the outcome?

In order to answer these questions, you must examine your interest in a story idea very carefully. Your dramatic center is the best tool you have for ensuring that the plotline you develop will actually yield a screenplay that captures your excitement about the idea. Often the aspect of change that is connected with your dramatic center is hidden beneath the surface. For example, in my Lizzie script, the conflict might have seemed interpersonal, but it was really about societal repression. The film *The Duelist* seems to be about interpersonal conflict, yet it is really about the internal change that Keith Carradine's character needs to make in order to regain control of his life.

Like a surveyor, you want to be exact about identifying your dramatic center. If you are not, what could first seem like a minor inaccuracy at the center of your story will put you far off course later. Because this transition from raw creative impulse to concrete plot can be so challenging, let's examine one way to proceed that will ensure you stay on course.

■ The Pivotal Moment of Change ■

A good way to begin developing your plot is to determine exactly what the pivotal moment of change is in your story. The pivotal moment of change is the moment when the issues affecting the central change are resolved, leading to the external action that is the climax of the story.

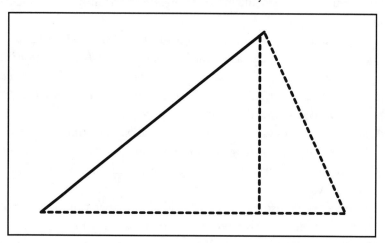

Figure 7-1   Pivotal Moment of Change

There is always a direct connection between your dramatic center and the pivotal moment of change. For example, if the dramatic center for my Lizzie Borden script is a fascination with her gradual move from sanity to insanity, the pivotal moment would occur when her sanity actually snaps. If my dramatic center is about her relation with her abusive father, the pivotal moment would be when she moves from being able to tolerate the abuse to being unable to control her rage any longer.

Your pivotal moment of change is the key moment you are building to, so once you know exactly where that is, you begin to have clarity about how to use your screen time. For example, if I were writing about Lizzie losing her mind, the information I would select from her story would be those details in which her sanity is more and more in doubt. If I were writing about her obtaining personal freedom from her abusive father, I would select the scenes in which his abuse becomes more and more intolerable. Even though the original source material for the two plotlines is the same, the selection from the entire spectrum of the story of events, characters, and moments would be quite different.

By using your dramatic center almost as the fulcrum of your pivotal moment, you can test the outcome against the visceral sensation signal, the beep-beep-beep of your dramatic center, to see how it feels. It's a firm, calm sense of clarity, and once you achieve it, you will feel your creative juices really starting to flow.

If you feel genuinely comfortable, then you are ready to go on to the next step. If not, stop now. Don't proceed. Instead, double-check your assessments and assumptions so far. No matter how annoying or unsettling it can be to force yourself to stay focused on these preliminary decisions, you will not be able to move ahead with confidence and clarity unless you are convinced you have a firm foundation.

■ The End Result ■

Once you feel that you have a grasp of the pivotal moment of change, the next step in developing your plotline is to extend your pivotal moment to see what the end result will be.

For example, in my Lizzie possibilities, the end result based on the pivotal moment in which she lost her sanity would present Lizzie as pitiable. In the other version, where she revolts against her father's abuse, she would feel triumphant about having ended the oppression that controlled her life. The external action of murder at the end of the story might be the same in both stories, but the emotional texture would be completely different.

Once you have tested your end result, you can ask whether that ending feels right to you. Is that the story you want to write? If so, you can move ahead with confidence. If not, chances are that you don't yet have complete clarity on your dramatic center or pivotal moment of change. So rather than push ahead, focus your energies on clarifying your dramatic center, and then test your findings until you find a pivotal moment and the end result that feels absolutely right. Try different variations until you feel total confidence that the plot that would result from these key moments makes the statement you want.

■ The Starting Point ■

The next step is to figure out where the plot should begin in order to make the ending feel emotionally and logically satisfying. The polarity between the starting point and the end result sets up the entire arc of your story. Therefore, choosing a beginning that allows the biggest change to occur is a good selection, because the more change that is necessary between the beginning and the end of the story, the more dramatic potential the story has.

In the two versions of the Lizzie story, for instance, the starting point for one would be while she was still quite sane; the other would start when she was abjectly fearful of her father. I may not yet know what the external "packaging" is of the scene, how I am going to dramatize Lizzie's sanity at the beginning of the screenplay, or the pivotal loss of sanity near the end. Once I can envision the emotional longitude and latitude of my story, I have real clarity about what emotional information I am trying to convey to the audience. Therefore I can begin to select plot events with a clear function in mind.

■ The Dramatic Equation ■

Now you have three key moments in the plotline: the starting point, the pivotal moment of change, and the end result. Feeling genuinely confident about the implied boundaries of your story is crucial, because your plot is a major ingredient in the dramatic equation of your story.

The dramatic equation of a story is its message or statement of values. Boiled down to its essence, your script conveys the message "this person plus this change inevitably equals this outcome."

Like an algebraic equation, the internal dynamics of a story must add up and make sense. For example, in *Dead Man Walking*, Susan Sarandon's character as a nun, plus her encounters with a specific death row prisoner and the people whose lives he affected, ultimately lead to her change of values and even life priorities.

In well-crafted short films the dramatic equation is very clear, as it is in short stories. In longer films the central equation is not always so obvious, but the internal logic behind the series of changes must still hold up in order for the audience to feel a sense of clarity and completion. Viewers may not be conscious of the equation. In fact, they usually aren't unless they try to articulate their thoughts about the film. If they do, you may be surprised by how clearly viewers register the central statement of your film.

There's also an important issue of integrity regarding the dramatic equation. You will not feel fully confident unless you believe that the implied statement of your story is essentially true. Even if it's just a comic romp, there is an implied statement of relative values in every screenplay. If you don't believe the logic, world view, and values expressed in your story, internal doubt will cause repeated problems, including creative resistance and even "shutdown."

■ Selecting Your Story Pillars ■

If you are sure that you have defined the boundaries of your story successfully, the next step is selecting and arranging story events so that a series of changes propels the audience from your starting point to the end result. That accumulation of story information combines to create your dramatic equation.

For example, if I were dramatizing Lizzie and her father, by now I would have a clear sense of the underlying tension between them. I would then have to decide what would be the best way to present that information to the audience. Should they fight frequently? Live in stoic silence? Does Lizzie reach out for contact while her father turns his back? Keeping the central function in mind as you explore possibilities will allow your mind to create the most exciting and compelling packaging, because the internal criterion is clear.

Sometimes the external packaging comes to mind first, and you have to search for the deeper issues. Other times, the central change is clear, but exactly what events will best dramatize it is harder to decide. Once you have made your decisions, that information will be conveyed to the audience in *story pillars*—the pieces of information that cause change within the story.

The change may affect the character's status quo (a woman is hit by a car), the character's understanding of the status quo (the woman learns she is dying), the audience's understanding of the status quo (the audience learns that she is dying but she doesn't know), or any combination of the three. The difference between general plot information and a story pillar is that the story pillars must cause the sensation of change or potential change. Events such as characters brushing their teeth or driving in their cars are not story pillars unless they contain information that might affect the central dynamic of change.

A story pillar's height comes from the intensity of audience reaction; the intensity comes from how much possible change could result from the new information. For example, you might think that a scene in which a building burns down is innately more intense than a scene in which a waitress casually declines an offer to have coffee with a customer. However, the burning building could generate no emotional response from viewers if they already know it's on fire. Meanwhile, the scene with the waitress may break your heart if you know that she and the customer are in love and that she will never see him again because he is planning to commit suicide. The power of the second scene comes from the fact that both of their lives will be irrevocably changed by the seemingly small moment.

The sensation I get when a moment of potential change occurs is similar to watching a wall in a Las Vegas casino that displays the numerical odds. Every time a story pillar suggests that there will be a shift, the numbers on the wall flip—sometimes higher, sometimes lower—reflecting the audience's assessment of whether the story's central conflict will be successfully resolved or not. The higher the pillar, the more the numbers change. When the story pillar contains information that results in a small change, only a few numbers flip. In the really big moments of change, it can seem as though the entire wall of numbers is changing!

■ Arranging Your Pillars ■

Once you are clear on what your key pillars are, you need to start thinking about how to arrange them. You must align them, both in terms of the internal logic of the story line and the emotional height. For example, you may have a clear sense that your character has a major argument with a neighbor. You also you need to decide whether that argument should happen before or after the character's other argument with the letter carrier. Your decision will depend on which scene you expect to be more intense.

You won't be able to set these in stone until other creative decisions are also made, but as you think about the plot, keep in mind the image of growing pillars. If you isolate each pillar in your mind and try various arrangements, chances are that you will develop a visceral sense of which pillar is higher.

Another way to think of these load-bearing pillars is as *landmarks of change.* By tracking them the audience can understand both the pressures toward change, and how far those pressures have advanced in your plotline. The total pattern of landmarks of change should combine to create an increasingly difficult "obstacle course." As you continue to develop your plot, you should achieve clarity about what kind of obstacle course your plotline offers, and exactly what kind of people would find it most challenging. That inherent connection between plot and characters will have tremendous impact on how you will develop your story, as we will see in the next chapter.

■ Increasing the Height of Your Pillars ■

There are seven approaches that can give pillars added height. They involve how much is at stake, how much jeopardy exists, how significant the obstacle is, how desperate or unpredictable the situation is, how the pattern of change is developing, or how much the audience understands about the situation. Let's take them one at a time.

1. Increasing Dramatic Stakes

One way you get the load-bearing pillars of your plot to become higher is by increasing the *dramatic stakes,* which are what will be gained or lost in the encounter with change.

Dramatic stakes can be positive, such as gaining money, as in *The Great Train Robbery,* gaining love, as in *Four Weddings and a Funeral,* or gaining freedom, as in "Murder One" or *Europa, Europa.* Dramatic stakes can also be negative, as in *Executive Decision,* where many people will lose their lives if they fail, while in *The Terminator,* the entire human race could be destroyed if the challenge is not successfully met.

2. Increasing Jeopardy

You can also achieve added height by increasing the *jeopardy,* as in Steven Spielberg's television movie *Duel,* in which a small incident on a desert highway eventually becomes a life-and-death battle.

It's important to remember that all jeopardy doesn't have to be physical; emotional violence can be equally gripping, as seen in films like *Gaslight.* The impending change can also switch from emotional intensity to physical attacks, as in *The Hand That Rocks the Cradle,* in which a nanny bent on revenge first makes emotional assaults before her attacks turn physical.

Another way you can increase jeopardy is by revealing that the source of opposition is more powerful than originally thought, as in *All the President's Men, Witness,* and *Chinatown.*

3. Increasing Obstacles

You can also add height to story pillars by adding to the *number of obstacles* that threaten to prevent successful encounters with change.

One way to build pillar height is to increase the numbers of opponents, as in *Night of the Living Dead* or *The Birds.* Comedies use a similar dynamic with multitudes of small problems compounding the main problem, as in *Bringing Up Baby, The Out-of-Towners,* and *The In-Laws.* Another variation occurs when the sources of danger continue to escalate no matter what evasive action is taken, as in *The Anderson Tapes,* in which it feels like most of New York's police force eventually surround an apartment building that Sean Connery and his crew are robbing.

4. Increasing Desperation

You can also add pillar height by increasing the urgency of the situation. This is often referred to as a "ticking clock," meaning that the situation will definitely get worse with time.

One variation is to make sure the audience knows that time is running out, as in *The Andromeda Strain* or *High Noon.* Other variations include the declining strength of the hero, as in *Dog Day Afternoon* and *The Shootist,* or increasing proximity of danger, as in *Independence Day* and *The Eye of the Needle,* or declining resources, as in *Alive* or *Lifeboat.*

Increasing desperation can also be created by *shutting doors,* in which possible solutions are eliminated one by one. This technique was used in *Alien* and *Outland,* in which various groups of people, options, or equipment that were supposed to support the characters failed to do so.

5. Increasing Unpredictability

Plot twists that make events increasingly unpredictable are another way to add height to the pillars of your roller coaster. They are key moments of change where the direction or speed of your roller coaster suddenly shifts. Just as riders of a real roller coaster stop moving forward but feel as though they are still moving ahead, plot twists provide exciting sensations for viewers.

Plot twists may occur when the opponent becomes increasingly unstable, as in the computer Hal's behavior in *2001; A Space Odyssey,* Bette Davis in

Whatever Happened to Baby Jane, Natural Born Killers, or Kramer's behavior in "Seinfeld." Unpredictability can also be caused by a *discovery,* which is a piece of information that changes the significance of previous information, as in *House of Games.* A *reversal* occurs when the audience learns that their previous assumption is the exact opposite of the truth, as in *The Conversation* or *No Way Out.*

When using plot twists, it's important to ask yourself what expectations you must create in the audience's mind in order to get the full dramatic power out of your plot twists. Such changes have to be well integrated into the rest of the story or the audience will feel manipulated or cheated.

6. Increasing Likelihood of Change

Another way to increase pillar height is through a sense of *implied build,* which means that the audience, consciously or subconsciously, begins to sense a pattern of difficulties that suggests that the pattern will continue.

One effective pattern is *quicksand,* in which the troubles become more and more enveloping, as in *Double Indemnity, Malice,* or the comedies *What About Bob?* and *The Money Pit. Step by step* occurs when the audience can see a pattern but the character isn't yet fully aware, as in *Reds, Psycho,* or the TV movie *Sybil.* Tracking the cumulative changes in such films provides a lot of emotional power even though the individual incidents may seem small.

7. Increasing Revelations

The more the audience understands the possible ramifications of an event, the more emotional impact the event can have on viewers. Therefore, another important technique to build pillar height is often not to make the series of events onscreen more intense, but simply to increase the significance of the information that the audience already has about the event.

For example, a frightened man sitting alone in a room may not seem too dramatic, so often writers will try to heighten the impact by having the character pace frantically or some other intense action. However, such techniques can quickly become melodramatic. Instead, if you make sure that the audience fully understands the implications of what's happening, then they will supply all the drama that is needed within their own negative space. For example, if viewers know that the man's wife is a killer who has trapped him in this room and plans to murder him, the same still scene of the man in the room immediately becomes more powerful. When he hears a key in the door, the emotional reaction in viewers' negative space becomes even more intense. One of the reasons that *Body Heat* is so powerful is the contrast between the seemingly small bits of information that occur in the second half of the film, compared to the magnitude of betrayal the information suggests.

■ Designing Dips ■

Just because the overall pattern of pillars must increase doesn't mean that each individual pillar must be higher than the last. As we've discussed before, you can design any kind of roller coaster you want, as long as you are in control of where and how the highs and lows take place.

An intentional dip can be very effective emotionally, as in the film *The Fugitive*. After the powerhouse opening, the slower paced segment in which Harrison Ford is working in the hospital to get information seems to be an intentional change of intensity so the story can build up again for the final climax. The television show "Columbo" has used this structure for years. The first spike represents the murder that the audience watches in the first act; then the tension temporarily subsides as Columbo makes his entrance, after which it starts to build again.

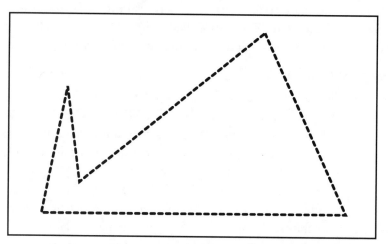

Figure 7-2   Intentional Dip Roller Coaster

While films such as *The Day of the Jackal* get much of their power from an almost linear ascending structure, audiences often need a resting place to catch their breath or get oriented before the next change occurs. Short scenes of quiet time or comic relief can fulfill this function. Many horror films use quiet moments between attacks in order to make the upward surge of audience energy more exciting by contrast, as did the film *Alive,* in which the survivors of a plane crash which occurs quite early in the movie then endure an alternating series of terrifying crises and haunting stillness.

■ The Connection Between Plot and Structure ■

As you continue developing your plot, you will see that the pattern created by connecting the top of your various story pillars reflects the structure. Since the height of these pillars is determined by the intensity of the audience's emotional reaction to information, you should arrange pillars according to your best guess as to how strongly the audience will react. The height you choose for your pillars is a statement—your opinion—of their relative value.

Additionally, just as the top line of your story pillars becomes your structure, the sequence of the story pillars on the bottom line becomes the logical progression of the plot. Therefore, having some sense of the overall structure you are trying to create with your plot is very useful once you identify the emotional pattern you are trying to achieve.

For instance, if you were trying to build your roller coaster with a "big bang" opening, the height of the first story pillar would be created by the audience's reactions to a vicious murder, an exciting car chase, a plane crash, or whatever story event is most suitable to your storyline.

This visual image can be a tremendously useful tool for a writer because it gives you a tangible gauge by which to measure your story. It's not enough to ask yourself, "Which event occurs next?" You should also ask, "How high does the pillar need to be?" or "How can I achieve the height this scene needs?" The trick is to make sure that each significant story pillar gets higher, and that the overall pattern is in keeping with your visceral sense of what the structure should be.

■ A Word About Subplots ■

As the name implies, a secondary plot is not essential to the story, but it offers the audience additional information about the central events, explaining or illuminating factors that affect the main storyline. Often subplots do this by contrasting with the main story, or sometimes by enriching the main plot by examining key characters' motives, feelings, and decisions.

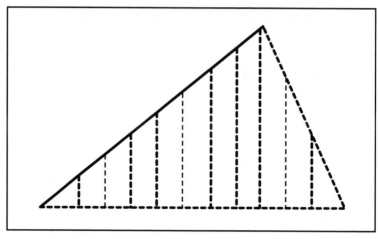

Figure 7-3   Subplots

You should arrange your subplot story pillars in terms of chronology, logic, and pillar height. It's important to make a clear decision about what your plotline is and what is secondary. Otherwise, issues affecting the central plotline are often underdramatized, while the secondary plot gets too much screen time. Even if you are telling an ensemble story with multiple but equally important storylines, a clear vision of your intended cinematic roller-coaster ride will give your story a sense of unity and cohesion. Otherwise, you can end up with an erratic, choppy structure that does not build coherently to a clear climax and resolution. Another frequent problem is a subplot that peaks too soon, making the main plot look anticlimactic. That's what almost happened in *An Officer and a Gentleman*. If you think you may be confronting this kind of problem, try arranging the story pillars of your secondary plots in a variety of ways to ensure they are most effectively integrated into your overall roller coaster.

Subplots should contain at least a starting point, a pivotal moment of change, and an end result, but should not contain as many intervening landmarks of change, and therefore do not demand as much screen time as the main plot. In Chapter Nine, we will talk more about this topic, but in general the more clarity you have on your dramatic center and intended structure, the more effectively you can enhance them through use of supporting elements.

Despite its obvious importance, plot is not the only ingredient in a successful screenplay. In the next chapter, let's begin looking at characters to see how that story dynamic fits into the overall cinematic roller coaster.

Q U E S T I O N S

1. What type of change are you writing about?
   Internal?
   Interpersonal?
   Societal?
   Situational?

2. What pattern of change intrigues you?
   Can you find a relationship between that pattern, your structure, and the sequence of key story pillars?

3. How does it relate to your dramatic center?

4. How does that relate to your overall structure?

5. Do you have a clear sense of the overall roller coaster you are trying to build?

6. How does your plot provide conflict resolution?
   Help viewers bond to the story?
   Supply new information?
   Provide a sense of completion?

7. What is the pivotal moment of change?
   End result?
   Starting point?
   Landmarks of change?

8. What is your dramatic equation?

9. Do your plot and structure necessarily result in your dramatic center?

10. How do you increase the height of your pillars?
    Increasing dramatic stakes?
    Increasing obstacles?
    Increasing desperation?
    Increasing likelihood of change?
    Increasing knowledge?

11. What kind of obstacle course is your plot creating?

12. Have you designed any "dips" in your roller coaster?

Characters: Getting the Audience on Board

Now you've designed your roller coaster and built the pillars to support it. However, in order for it to create a compelling experience, you must get people on board. Luring the audience onto your story roller coaster is the function of *characters*, who express emotions that provoke a sense of recognition in viewers.

The resulting connection between the story and the audience is created through the recognition of *universal emotions*, the primal, almost archetypal sensations at the root of any emotional experience. For example, the feeling of "not enough" is the same sensation at its core, whether it's not having enough money to buy food when you're hungry or not having enough money to save a tycoon's vast business empire. If audiences were only able to relate to specifics of a plot, they would be interested solely in stories that duplicated the specific events and dilemmas of their own lives. However, through the recognition of universal emotions, which serve as a common denominator between the story and the audience, viewers can relate to a character's dilemma by using their own experiences as a point of reference.

The audience hooks up with your story through the characters mainly because characters address the four basic audience needs. Universal emotions allow the audience to *bond* with the story, which is the central emotional need addressed by characters. Characters also address the audience's need for *new information* through unusual personalities, habits, attitudes, or philosophies. This can be seen in *Evita*, *Apollo Thirteen*, "The X-Files," or "Third Rock from the Sun." Audiences satisfy their need for *conflict resolution* by observing how characters deal with their problems. Characters also address the need for *completion*, which is why creating emotional arcs that make sense and move convincingly from beginning to end is so important to an audience's overall satisfaction with a story.

There are three categories of characters—heroes, antagonists, and secondary characters. Each provokes a different dynamic in the audience and fulfills a distinct function within the story's dramatic equation. Let's look at each in detail. Heroes will be examined in this chapter; antagonists and secondary characters will follow in the next.

Heroes and Heroines

Heroes and heroines (for the sake of brevity, both will be referred to as heroes) are an expression of, and feed the hunger for, the highest aspirations of human nature and life-affirming values, as in *The Shawshank Redemption*. Heroes also provide an antidote to the audience's sense of daily frustration. Viewers get a vicarious thrill out of watching the hero say and do things that people are reluctant to do in real life. Because one definition of courage is the ability to accept change and to act appropriately, the most important criteria for defining heroes is that they must know, or learn, the truth, and then they must act or accept the consequences of inaction.

Audiences are fascinated by how or why people change, so they are eager for role models of wisdom and courage. Whether courage is tested in a big action/adventure like *The Rock* or in a quiet moment of truth as in *Twelve O'Clock High*, viewers find watching someone trying to take the "high road" inspirational, even when that effort fails.

Sometimes heroes express their truths physically, as in *Cliffhanger*. Sometimes they express themselves orally, as Peter Finch does in *Network* or as Robin Williams does in *Good Morning, Vietnam*. Sometimes they act with great reluctance, as in *The Quiet Man*, and sometimes with passion, as in *Gandhi*. Whatever form it takes, a hero must be faced with the decision to take action by the end of the story, even if the decision leads to a failure to act, as in *The Bridges of Madison County*.

■ Rooting Interest ■

Audiences will enjoy a story more if they actually have an emotional stake in the outcome. Effective heroes generate a strong sense of *rooting interest*. That means the audience cares greatly about what happens to them and whether or not they achieve their goals.

Similar to the gamblers at a racetrack, viewers will enjoy the race and get much more emotionally involved if they have money riding on who wins. It's a feeling of personalized investment, as if viewers have chosen the hero as their favorite horse. The result is that if the hero wins, the viewers win.

Developing rooting interest depends on three dynamics:

1. The audience must want the hero to win,

2. They must think the hero is capable of winning, and

3. They must believe the hero deserves to win.

Many writers interpret the first criterion as making the hero likable. However, that's not inclusive enough because it is possible to develop rooting interest for characters the audience doesn't like. The only real necessity is that the audience must feel empathy with the character. They need to make a connection with the hero's motives, methods, feelings, and/or situation, or any other elements that create a sense of recognition, allowing the character to serve as the viewers' "emotional proxy."

The second consideration for developing rooting interest is that the audience must believe that the hero is capable of winning. To put it another way, the audience simply will not bond with a hero they suspect has no chance of success. As in real life, people are protective of their emotions, especially if those emotions could be powerful and sad. Audiences won't bond with a hero unless there is a reasonable chance of an uplifting experience, so even in films like *Leaving Las Vegas*, the audience keeps hoping that Nicholas Cage's attachment to his girlfriend will convince him not to die.

For rooting interest to form, audiences should think the hero deserves to win. Somewhere in the story, the hero needs to demonstrate at least one characteristic that provides a legitimate reason for admiration. That development usually occurs when the hero acts in a way that genuinely impresses the audience. It is that transcendence of normal inhibition that often defines the hero.

It is a mistake to think that a hero is created or defined by eventual success in the game. Real heroism comes from being willing and able to go into battle. The audience might prefer that the hero win, but only because they feel bonded to the character. It's entirely possible to be a compelling hero and still lose the final fight, as in *Braveheart,* which featured one of the most compelling and well-defined heroes in many years.

■ Matchup of Hero and Obstacle Course ■

Many writers think that the excitement in a story comes directly from the obstacles in the plot or the personality of the hero, but the real excitement is created by the matchup between the hero and the obstacles. For example, crossing a street before the light changes doesn't seem like much of a challenge, especially if the hero is an Olympic runner. However, change the hero to a physically disabled five-year-old boy determined to get across the street without taking his mother's hand, and suddenly the same challenge is riveting.

All the criteria for rooting interest are profoundly affected by the matchup between the hero and the obstacle course. The matchup depends on two factors—the absolute difficulty of the challenge and the hero's relative *level of ability to deal with change*. Therefore it is critical that you understand your hero's basic level of ability and what kind of change would be the most difficult for the character. As in *Vertigo*, the story has to contain a plot that presents the most challenging "obstacle course," thus creating the most exciting matchup to the character's abilities. Any contest that is too easy or too hard will destroy the balance and tension needed to create a compelling story.

Understanding each hero's level of ability and attitude towards change can help you define what each hero needs to do to earn the audience's respect. It will also help you clarify and define the hero's character arcs, the core of the hero's emotional bond with viewers, and how to use your screen time to give the audience the information they need for the hero to be the most effective.

Four Types of Heroes

There are four types of heroes, all of which are defined by their level of ability of skill and capacity to deal with change.

The following categories are not meant to be absolute, but to help you identify and create the dynamics needed for the audience to genuinely root for the hero's success. Each type of hero helps the audience bond to the positive space of a story in different ways, and each one contributes to a different kind of roller coaster design. Yet all four types provoke powerful life-affirming sensations in the viewers' negative space, which is what creates the sense of heroism.

1. The Idol Hero

An Idol hero is someone whose abilities are usually much higher than the average person's, but the defining quality of Idol heroes is their lack of self doubt, ambivalence, or inner confusion. In many ways, James Bond represents both the total confidence and superior skills that an Idol hero can have. Idol heroes don't have to be perfect or even physically impressive. For example, the pompous Hercule Poirot or elderly Miss Marple are Idol heroes because of their complete lack of self doubt.

The Idol hero takes actions that are not only appropriate, but often inspired. Much of the Idol hero's appeal is his or her surprising knowledge and inventiveness, especially under pressure. Idol heroes know the truth right away, have no doubts about their assessment, and take action without hesitation.

Needless to say, that is very different from what most people experience in their daily lives. The audience doesn't identify with Idol heroes' lack of ambiguity as much as they recognize their own desire to have that kind of unshakable confidence. As a result, bonding with such heroes provides a vacation from inner turmoil and confusion.

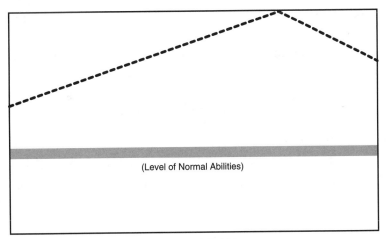

(Level of Normal Abilities)

Figure 8-1   Idol Hero

Despite their amazing confidence, these heroes do not need to be perfect. For example, *The Thin Man* showcases William Powell and Myrna Loy as Idol heroes. They are cavalier, never second-guess themselves, never hesitate to take risks, and do everything with complete panache. Idol heroes may be exceptional when dealing with their expertise, but they can have flaws and foibles. Often Idol heroes have endearing imperfections, such as Superman's bashful behavior as Clark Kent, or Arnold Schwarzenegger's lack of social cool and hip talk in *Terminator 2: Judgement Day*, which was then supplied by the boy he saves.

A successful Idol hero may even have substantial failings, such as Sherlock Holmes' use of cocaine. The key factor is to make sure such decorative characteristics do not detract from the Idol heroes' ability to use their skills with strength and precision, nor their ability to perform flawlessly in their major arena. It can be a crucial mistake to allow Idol heroes' quirks and foibles to affect their performance. A James Bond who agonizes over every action loses his appeal, because it is primarily his confidence that makes the character attractive and fun.

Idol heroes do not undergo major emotional arcs because they begin and end as heroes. Therefore, they work well in stories concerned with outer conflict and change. These heroes act on behalf of justice, usually have a purpose beyond an immediate goal and are faithful in the service to which they are committed. Idol heroes are a driving force because they decide to be one. Because Idol heroes have skills and abilities much higher than the average person's, the obstacles they face must be much tougher than ordinary to create an exciting matchup.

Former film stars such as Clark Gable, John Wayne, and Marlene Dietrich exuded this sense of sublime self acceptance and lack of self doubt. These days, Clint Eastwood and Arnold Schwarzenegger are among the stars whose major film successes have basically positioned them as Idols.

2. The Everyman Hero

Unlike the Idol hero whose abilities and exploits are far above the average person's, the Everyman hero lives and struggles right in the thick of those everyday challenges. The core of the audience's emotional bond is that they see this hero as a peer, with strengths and weaknesses similar to their own. The same things that are hard for the audience are difficult for this kind of hero. The defining element that identifies an Everyman hero is the "peer bond" with viewers created through a sense of recognition and identification. Some examples of these heroes can be seen in *The Honeymooners, The Way We Were, Hannah and Her Sisters, Courage Under Fire, Poltergeist, North by Northwest, The First Wives Club, The Truth about Cats and Dogs, and* "Grace Under Fire," "Ellen," and "Friends."

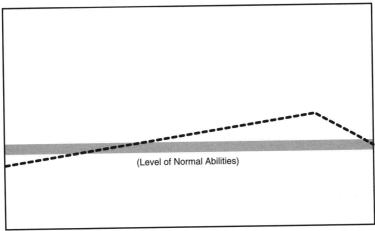

(Level of Normal Abilities)

Figure 8-2   Everyman Hero

Many film stars have made careers from playing this kind of role. Steve Martin, Henry Fonda, Jimmy Stewart, Bette Davis, Jean Harlow, Harrison Ford, Sandra Bullock, Tom Hanks, Emma Thompson, Winona Ryder, Kevin Costner, Jody Foster, Mel Gibson, Tom Cruise, and Michael Douglas have all excelled in these kinds of roles. Many comedic actors, such as Bob Newhart, Mary Tyler Moore, Dick Van Dyke, and Bill Murray, also convey this kind of energy. Much of Marilyn Monroe's charm was the combination of out-of-this-world sex appeal combined with a very accessible, identifiable Everyman charm.

Unlike the Idol hero, these heroes usually have many doubts, and they become heroes only when they are able to rise above the doubt and confusion to act. The audience will be patient as long as they believe (1) the inner conflict is real, (2) the search for the truth is genuinely difficult, (3) the hero is really trying, and (4) the hero will take action once the truth is learned. (However, if the character takes a long time to find the truth and then stalls before taking action, the audience will feel cheated because the character failed to act heroically.)

The Everyman hero can find it very difficult to face the need to accept change and/or act on it. Often the challenges within the story reveal the truth to this hero, and a large part of the heroism is finding a way to accept it, despite the inconvenience, pain, and difficult change it may demand. Despite their many flaws and weaknesses, Everyman heroes are able to rise above those limitations, at least for a moment, to take control of the situation. The audience is fascinated by the mechanics of real heroism, which has been defined as "not the absence of fear, but acting despite the fear." Like the grandmother who somehow finds the strength to lift the car off her trapped grandchild, these heroes have moments of glorious triumph although they don't live their lives in such a state.

Bonding with the Everyman hero gives viewers a chance to affirm and synchronize their emotions, as discussed in Chapter Two. These heroes live in a world of doubt, confusion, and ambiguity, and their story is their struggle to rise above that. Their heroism comes from overcoming internal issues in order to influence the outside world.

Everyman heroes are life-affirming, because they convey the message that a person doesn't have to be perfect, or brilliant, to succeed. These heroes change through the story, usually because they learn a lesson. Often they start out thinking better of themselves than they deserve; if there is a discrepancy between what the characters think and do, it is more common that they overestimate themselves. For example, in *Kramer vs. Kramer*, Dustin Hoffman's character thinks he's a swell father and husband at the beginning of the story. It's only through the flow of events that he comes to reevaluate his abilities, becoming a hero because he is willing to act on the truths he discovers.

Most genre pieces (such as cop, detective, or horror films, Westerns, and love stories) have Everyman heroes because they are the easiest hero with which viewers can bond. Alfred Hitchcock made a career of directing films that have been described as "ordinary people in extraordinary situations." Everyman heroes tend to become a driving force in the story because of their own need for peace or resolution. Because their heroism is defined by facing and accepting the truth despite the pain, it is crucial that the audience have a clear understanding of how much pain they are feeling, and what acting on their truths may cost.

Bruce Willis' character in *Die Hard* is an excellent example of an Everyman hero. He is determined to overcome seemingly impossible odds. However, enough screen time is spent on his frustrations, sense of desperation, and physical pain that the audience fully understands what internal obstacles he is overcoming in order to resolve the external dilemma.

3. The Underdog Hero

Underdog heroes are characters at a genuine disadvantage when compared to the world around them. Their handicaps can be physical, emotional, social, or mental. They also must be legitimate in the character's estimation as well as the audience's, so that viewers will accept that this type of hero is working from a genuine disadvantage that must be overcome.

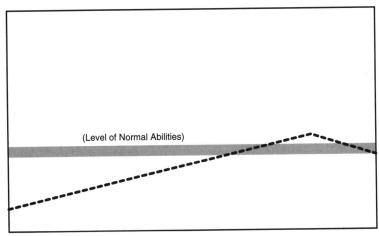

(Level of Normal Abilities)

Figure 8-3   Underdog Hero

Underdogs become heroes by triumphing over these seemingly insurmountable obstacles in a way that lets them take control of their lives. Some examples are *Rocky, Gaslight, Raising Arizona, My Left Foot, Forrest Gump, The Jerk, Life Goes On,* and *The Mighty Ducks.* Many actors make a career creating this kind of character, including Chris Farley, Pauly Shore, Charlie Chaplin, Johnny Depp, and Jim Carrey, as well as many roles played by Dustin Hoffman, Joan Crawford, and Jimmy Cagney.

These heroes have great ambiguity, and generally underestimate themselves. Part of their potential for heroism is that they are much more capable of change than they realize. Underdogs can start out as losers, but there must be some indication to the audience that the Underdogs can win, even if they don't believe it themselves. Planting seeds of greatness in the characterization of an Underdog is important because the audience will not bond with a character who has no chance of winning. The Underdog must have potential to win, even if the circumstances and odds are against it.

These heroes often know the truth early, and their heroism comes from sticking to that truth even when the appropriate action is hard. An example would be stroke victims who know they want to walk again; their heroism comes from their repeated efforts to succeed, despite all obstacles. Everyone knows how hard it is to stay on a diet, or save money, or stand up to the boss, so it's easy to admire a character who overcomes even greater challenges, like a stroke. The example of courage despite overwhelming odds is what makes the Underdog hero life-affirming to the audience. Screen time spent ensuring the audience knows the handicap is genuine will heighten these characters' appeal. It's also important to use screen time to emphasize the Underdog hero's tenacity and discipline because it makes the accomplishments even more impressive.

Underdogs become heroes when they conquer their internal obstacles long enough to overcome external obstacles. They are not usually a driving force in the story until pushed to be by outside circumstances. As in *Karate Kid*, they finally change because they are unwilling to endure the pain of remaining the same any longer.

These heroes usually know what they want early in the story, but have to find the strength to achieve it or even to believe that it is possible. Their goal is usually expressed by an external challenge, such as trying to walk again after the stroke, but the more difficult challenge is the conquest of their internal doubts, discouragement, and fears. Underdogs often change over the course of a story, especially in their view of themselves. If there is a discrepancy between how they see themselves and how the world sees them, these heroes will often think more poorly of themselves than others do. These heroes, therefore, are usually involved in transformation stories. Underdog heroes gain new ability, or new understanding of their ability, through the obstacle course of the story.

4. The Lost Soul Hero

The heroes we have discussed so far create a bond with the audience through positive emotions, but the Lost Soul hero connects with the darker side of human nature. These heroes express an aspect of life that viewers rarely want to talk about or deal with. Audiences almost admire these heroes' courage to be bad, because they are not stopped by personal morality or by fear of the consequences like most of us. Some examples of Lost Souls are seen in *Damage, Anna Karenina, The Story of Adele H., Bonnie and Clyde, Amadeus, Sugarland Express, Raging Bull, Citizen Kane*, as well as the younger brothers in *A River Runs Through It* and *The Mambo Kings*, while some actors who often portray this kind of hero are Brad Pitt, Robert DiNero, and Nicholas Cage.

Viewers don't bond with these heroes through their highest hopes and dreams, but rather by recognizing some of their own darkest, most secret fears. From the audience's point of view, this is a peer who takes the wrong turn, often eliciting a "There but for the grace of God go I" sensation. This ultimately forces viewers to abandon their emotional identification with Lost Soul heroes when they go too far into the dark corners of life.

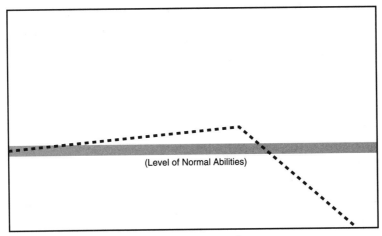

Figure 8-4   Lost Soul Hero

These kinds of heroes are life-affirming not because of the actions they take in the "positive space" of the story, but because of the sensations within the audience's "negative space." Initially, the audience has the guilty feeling that they, too, would make the same choices when the crimes aren't too bad; after all, it's fun to have the dark side released temporarily. Individually, this hero's decisions and actions must make sense, or seem acceptable at first, as in *Interview with a Vampire*. Slowly the character's path begins to go astray, and the crimes become more serious. These heroes' desires may not be admirable, but they must be understandable. If the audience can't imagine wanting the same things, viewers' eventual rejection of this character will be less intense and emotionally powerful.

Eventually, though, the hero goes one step too far, and viewers pullback; they experience a sense of relief and personal encouragement that they are not bad after all. They feel they have better moral or ethical judgment than the character; indeed, in their negative space, the audience feels superior.

The last scene in *The Godfather* is a perfect example of this dynamic. When Michael Corleone chooses to lie to his wife, it signals a complete reversal of the values that he held at the beginning of the story. As the camera pulls back, leaving him to face the future he has chosen alone, the visual image represents the same dynamic that is occurring in the audience's minds.

The final rejection of the Lost Soul's actions and values, when viewers abandon the Lost Soul to the dark path as they return to the light, is what makes this hero both dramatic and life-affirming. Because of the previously established bond between these heroes and the audience, viewers have a sense of loss or mourning as they leave these heroes to face their bleak fate alone.

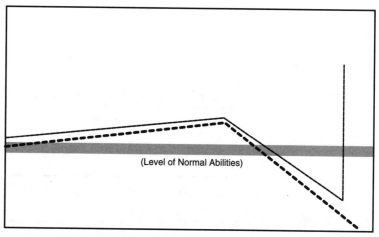

(Level of Normal Abilities)

Figure 8-5   Audience Reaction to Lost Soul

These heroes change as the story progresses, but always in a downward direction. The cause of this negative change is the avoidance of the change, ignoring the truth, failure to act on it, or taking inappropriate actions. Often these heroes have a chance to learn a moral lesson that could save them (and secondary characters in such stories often learn that lesson and pull out in time), but these heroes either can't or won't. The audience does, which only heightens the sense of regret or even tragedy that the hero can't find the right path.

■ Which Hero Is Right for Your Story? ■

Determining which hero is right for your story depends on your dramatic center. What kind of change do you want to dramatize? What kind of roller coaster are you trying to build? A story about small, incremental changes may need an Underdog hero, while a story about big-scale action battles may demand the strengths and abilities of an Idol.

The hero's level of ability to deal with change is also a crucial factor in expressing the dramatic equation of your story. What kind of events force your hero into crisis? Why are those changes especially hard for this hero to accept? If you have a clear sense of what dramatic equation you want your story to convey, it will help you determine just how strong the hero should be and what kind of abilities your hero should have. You must become very conscious about what kind of hero you are creating and why that hero is ideally suited to your plot's obstacle course so that you can use your screen time to communicate that information to viewers.

■ Making Your Hero More Effective ■

Here are some techniques for making your hero more effective:

1. Separate the Hero from "the World"

The hero should always be presented in contrast to, if not in conflict with, "the world" of the story. It is that separation that makes his or her story worth telling. For example, an advertising executive who loves his work and has no complaints about the company is not as interesting as an executive who hates working there and is plotting his escape.

The issue that separates the hero from the world is also crucial to your story because it is a tangible expression of the dramatic center of your script. For example, in my Lizzie play, it was her inability or unwillingness to be repressed any longer that eventually separated her from her world. Sometimes heroes are fully aware of these differences from the beginning of the story, as in *One Flew Over the Cuckoo's Nest*. Other heroes do not realize that crucial difference until the climactic moments of the story, as in *The Heiress*.

Sometimes this dynamic is called the "fish out of water" genre. Yet any story benefits from some element of polarity between the hero and the world. It conveys an inevitability of conflict that is structured into the central logic of the story. Without that clear distinction, the hero is weakened, and so is the overall dramatic equation of the story, as was seen in *Home for the Holidays* or *Mixed Nuts*. Every story is strengthened by the implied conflict. The more the element of separation is explored, the stronger the hero will seem, because the ability to hold to one's beliefs despite peer pressure is really the essence of heroism.

You can also intensify the audience's awareness of this polarity by your choice of *story arena*. Ask yourself how much you want to draw attention to the contrast, and then what arena would reflect the appropriate contrast. For example, the hero of *Working Girl* is more effective because the people of her world did not support her aspirations. Similarly, *Beverly Hills Cop* is more effective because it places Eddie Murphy in a posh setting. In his own world he still would have seemed like a nice guy, but since his values were in keeping with that world, he would have seemed much less special.

2. Establish a Personalized Link Between Hero and Audience

This idea is often stated as "Make your hero likable." This advice can be helpful if your hero's qualities are strengthened by making them more pleasant to spend time with. However, this rule is not absolute. Not only can it be quite limiting or incomplete, it can essentially gut your hero, especially if you are writing about Lost Soul heroes.

Another conventional wisdom is that you must create sympathy for the character, but, again, it's only a good technique for some types of heroes. It significantly undercuts the appeal of an Idol hero, for instance. Instead you should focus on making your hero *empathetic,* so that viewers feel a sense of recognition and affinity. An unsympathetic character whose feelings the audience understands is much more powerful than a sympathetic character whose simplistic emotions are too generic to provoke a genuine sense of bonding. This can often be seen in true life TV movies such as *The Executioner's Song.*

3. Establish the Hero's Strengths

Rooting interest should build over time as the audience learns about the characters. As the hero deals with continuing pressure, increasingly impressive qualities about him should become evident to the audience. As the obstacles get more and more serious, the audience needs to develop more reasons to have confidence in the hero, or they will lose confidence that the hero will be equal to the challenge.

A good example is *The Day of the Jackal.* The further the audience gets into the story, the more impressed they are with the hero's ability, even though eventually it becomes clear that he is a Lost Soul. Even when a hero is not such an expert, it is essential that he or she have at least one strength, a secret weapon, which makes it believable that he or she could win, no matter how terrifying the obstacle. That information can be obvious from the beginning, as with Idol heroes, or subtlety conveyed in "seeds of greatness" for an

Underdog. Regardless of how you address this in your script, never forget how crucial it is, for audiences won't bond with heroes unless they have a credible chance of success.

4. Establish the Hero's Vulnerability

A hero doesn't have to be perfect. In fact, except for an Idol hero, heroes need some significant internal or external challenge to overcome or their victories will seem too easy. It adds to the excitement of your story if there are real doubts about the hero's strengths, just as long as those vulnerabilities don't contradict the hero's essential appeal.

What is your hero's secret liability? The secret flaw—the Achilles' heel—is crucial to developing a well-rounded character. As you develop the central matchup, think about the events of your plotline and why they would have greater impact on your specific hero than on anyone else. For example, in *Arachnophobia,* the hero was phobic about spiders, which makes the dramatic stakes go up significantly.

5. Define the Hero's Values

Values are usually what separate heroes from their world, although sometimes they don't recognize this separation at the beginning of the story, as in *Tribute to a Bad Man.* Such values are often a statement of your dramatic center and are therefore a crucial element in the dramatic equation of your story.

6. Establish the Hero's Motives

In order for the audience to empathize with the hero, the audience must understand the hero's reasoning and private emotional desires. In *Anne of a Thousand Days,* for example, Henry VI is determined to have a male heir. Such motives are often connected to the dramatic stakes of your story and can either be positive ("I want to make more money") or negative ("I want to avoid being poor"). No matter how interesting the action scenes can be, without insight into the hero's inner motivations external "fireworks" can quickly lose their emotional power.

7. Establish the Hero's Goal

The hero's goal is always to complete the obstacle course successfully, but exactly what that means may not always be evident at the beginning of the story. Sometimes the obstacle course is apparent from the beginning of the script, as in *An Officer and a Gentleman;* sometimes the obstacle course emerges or becomes more difficult unexpectedly, as in *The Out-of-Towners*. The more the audience understands about the hero's intentions, the more they can identify with both the hero's triumphs and defeat.

8. Establish the Hero's Plan

Understanding the hero's plan and intended outcome also gives the audience the ability to measure the hero's success or failure along the way. The hero may have a clear plan from the very beginning, as in *The Great Train Robbery,* or the plan may develop in response to events as the story progresses, as in *Lorenzo's Oil*. Usually a great deal is revealed about the hero by how easily the plan is developed, executed, or how quickly a back-up plan can be created when things start to go wrong, as in *GoldenEye*.

9. Pearl of Battle

Recently I watched *The Scarlet Letter,* and the daughter created by that traumatic love affair was named Pearl. Similarly, in a well-constructed story the pivotal moment of change often forces heroes to reveal their true nature. These moments reveal not what the heroes think they are, or what the world thinks they are, or what they want the world to think they are. This is the moment of truth. Often this core truth would never have been produced except by the struggle, so it is the *pearl of battle,* the creation of beauty created by difficulty, as a pearl is the result of irritation in the oyster.

Q U E S T I O N S

These categories are not meant to be absolute. Rather, they are meant to start you thinking about your hero's level of ability so that you can make certain your hero will be well challenged by the events of your plot.

1. What kind of hero is best suited to your story?
   Idol?
   Everyman?
   Underdog?
   Lost Soul?
   Why?

2. What kind of change are you trying to dramatize?

3. What qualities do you need to spend your screen time establishing in order for the audience to bond with your hero?

4. What are the universal emotions that the audience can relate to in your hero's dilemma?
   How do you intend to show them?

5. Is there a good matchup between your hero and the obstacle course?
   What makes it an exciting contest?
   Why are your hero's strengths and weaknesses the best matchup for that obstacle course?

6. What kinds of skills does your hero have?
   Does your hero have seeds of greatness?
   An Achilles' heel?
   A clear motive?
   A goal?
   A plan?

7. What separates your hero and the world?
   What makes your hero distinctive?
   What sets your hero apart?

8. What values does your hero hold?
   How and/or why do they set your hero apart?
   Does your hero hold them at the beginning of the story?

9. Does your hero evolve from beginning to end?
   If so, why? How?

10. How does your hero address the need for new information?
    Bonding?
    Conflict resolution?
    Completion?

11. How does your hero rise (or fail to rise) to the occasion?
    What is the "pearl of battle"?

12. Have you safeguarded the core of your hero's appeal?

Creating Other Characters

We've seen how heroes fulfill their function of luring people onto a story roller coaster by expressing the desire for a positive encounter with change. However, not every human emotion is lofty, nor every desire pure. Other types of characters are needed besides heroes. These characters lure viewers on board your story roller coaster by giving them a chance to express and explore their negative emotions, their deepest fears, darkest angers, and morbid fantasies. Allowing the audience to vent such sensations is the function of *antagonists*, who represent the destructive or combative side of human nature.

Secondary characters are also important in fleshing out the dramatic equation of your story. Their major use is to help you dramatize the separation between the hero and the world. Having characters who function as friends, confidants, supporters, and romantic involvements helps personalize the disparity of values that are playing themselves out in the dramatic equation of your story.

Antagonists

A well-known industry saying claims that "Good villains make good movies." Creating a compelling film is not quite that simple, but it is true that many stories get their theatricality and power from the villain. While everyone can relate to the dreams and desires expressed by a hero character, having those desires thwarted is perhaps an even more universal experience. As a result, *antagonists* express the viewer's fear, frustration, and even nightmares, representing the forces of opposition. They provide antagonism, resistance, or the contrary force that creates an active battle between good and bad, right and wrong, productive and destructive.

Not every story needs to include a human antagonist. *The Old Man and the Sea* is an example of this. Others include *Being There, Diner,* or *How to Make an American Quilt.* Stories involving Lost Souls or internal conflicts also have no need for an antagonist since the heroes often carry the seeds of their own destruction inside them. However, even stories that don't employ the traditional "hero vs. antagonist" dynamic still benefit from having a personalized focus of opposition.

For example, in *Amadeus,* a brilliant examination of inner turmoil, the conflict and change facing Salieri were easier for the audience to grasp by placing Mozart in opposition. In reality, Mozart didn't cause Salieri's self-loathing, nor was there a struggle between the two men. Rather, the cause of the problem was Salieri's own inability to make peace with himself, a very personal (internal) struggle. Through Mozart's presence, Salieri—and the audience—became more conscious of Salieri's deficiencies and his corresponding discomfort with them.

When dramatizing situational change, as in *Dante's Peak* or the miniseries "Earthquake," there is no urgent need for a human antagonist because the real battle is against nature. Yet even in this kind of story, you will often find some secondary characters representing negative attitudes that help the audience personalize the threat, such as the reactions of different people in *Jurassic Park.*

Societal conflict can be personalized by inept officials as in *The China Syndrome,* the heartless lawyers in *Philadelphia,* ambitious scientists in *And The Band Played On,* or unforgiving relatives in *Dead Man Walking.* All of these characters present recognizable problems to help viewers relate to the almost unimaginable threats presented by the real opponents in these stories.

■ The Matchup of the Antagonist and the Hero ■

In many ways, heroes are defined by their struggle and can only be as interesting, compelling, or exciting as the forces they oppose. Antagonists are the representation of the forces against the hero, so they must be as overwhelming as possible because that is how viewers perceive their own problems.

The relative strength of the hero and the villain is a crucial element in your dramatic equation. The more powerful the antagonist, the stronger your hero will seem. In fact, powerful antagonists give stories much of their emotional impact because they represent the level of difficulty to which the hero must respond. Also, there is no suspense if the hero and the antagonist are not well matched, because there will be no doubt about who is going to win.

▪ The Three Kinds of Antagonists ▪

Just as heroes are defined by courage, antagonists are defined by how powerful they are, and how much they enjoy being destructive.

1. The Fiend

As seen through audience's eyes, the *Fiend* matches the Idol hero in ability, and even more importantly, in his or her lack of self doubt or ambivalence. Additionally, the Fiend's skill level is very high, if not superhuman. The Fiend is similar to the Idol hero in many ways; yet Fiends and Idols represent completely opposing moral values. The Fiend serves destruction while the Idol hero tries to build or preserve. In fact, Fiends actually enjoy destruction, whether it's to guarantee their own survival, as in *Dracula,* or for entertainment, as conveyed in Tim Roth's terrifying villain in *Rob Roy.* In comedies like *What About Bob?,* much of the humor comes from the Fiends' lack of sensitivity to social norms.

The essence of Fiend antagonists is that they are not stopped by the things that stop normal people, such as inner morality or social limits. That makes them more powerful, theatrical, extreme, and dangerous than many mainstream heroes. Some classic examples of Fiends are Freddie Krueger of the *Elm Street* movies, Dr. Moriarty in the Sherlock Holmes films, and Darth Vader in the *Star Wars* epics. Other examples are the shark in *Jaws,* the car in *Christine,* and Glenn Close in *Fatal Attraction.* Comic examples include William Powell in *Life with Father.*

When the battle is Idol vs. Fiend, there generally are large-scale events and major stakes, as in *Terminator 2: Judgement Day* or *Goldfinger.*

A Fiend vs. Everyman makes for an exciting contest, because it is very clear from the beginning that the hero is outmatched. That type of contest forces heroes to rise above their natural limits, at least for a few moments. Sharon Stone vs. Michael Douglas in *Basic Instinct* and the FBI agents against the supernatural in "The X-Files" are both matchups that create suspense about whether the heroes will be able to transcend their limitations. The Everyman becomes a genuine hero triumphing over the odds. *Die Hard, The Eye of the Needle,* and *The Silence of the Lambs* also offer examples of this matchup, and most horror films tend to be in this genre. Terrific humor can also be produced by a comic version of this matchup, as in Albert Brooks' *Mother.*

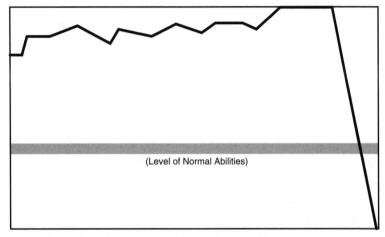

(Level of Normal Abilities)

Figure 9-1   Fiend

You don't often see a Fiend vs. an Underdog. The hero is so outmatched that the contest is hard to sustain. However, you can see this in some subplots, as in *The Wizard of Oz,* or with the cruel nanny against the mentally disabled gardener in *The Hand That Rocks the Cradle.* Additionally, *The Shining* first pits the Fiend played by Jack Nicholson against his wife, an Everyman hero. Then as his madness escalates, Nicholson attacks his young son, a classic Fiend/Underdog struggle.

2. The Adversary

Adversaries function at the same level of ability as Everyman, and are not necessarily evil; they just have a different agenda. These characters are the audience's equal in abilities and attitudes, and are just normal people—sometimes even good people—whose desires are in conflict with the hero's.

An Adversary vs. Idol is usually an unequal match unless there is a group of adversaries. *Robocop,* for example, pitted multiple Adversaries against an Idol hero.

An Adversary vs. Everyman tends to explore the more complex issues of the human condition, where there is no automatic right or wrong. Some examples are *Grumpy Old Men, When Harry Met Sally, Executive Decision,*

Adam's Rib, and *North by Northwest*. It is also common in genre films, like Westerns, detective stories, cop films, and love stories.

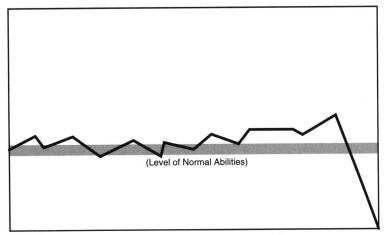

(Level of Normal Abilities)

Figure 9-2   Adversary

An Adversary vs. Underdog is often a comic device, as in *Babe, No Time for Sergeants*, or *The Pink Panther*.

3. The Pest

The Pest antagonist is very similar to the Underdog hero, in that they are not the audience's equal in innate power or personal ability. Pests get their power from their position or even proximity, and much of the trouble they cause is due to inappropriate use of their authority. Because of the low level of ability, this character is usually seen in comedies. It is also the least frequent type of antagonist because the Pest's ineptitude prevents a matchup with heroes of higher abilities from being exciting.

A Pest vs. Idol is quite a rare matchup. Because there is such a discrepancy in their abilities, you do not often see this matchup sustained throughout an entire story. However, one "partial" example would be Arnold Schwarzenegger versus the kids in *Kindergarten Cop*, although that's not what the story focuses on.

Pest vs. Everyman is much more frequent because it reflects the audience's own frustrations. Some examples are *Ferris Bueller's Day Off*, Albert Brook's *Mother*, and *Dennis the Menace*.

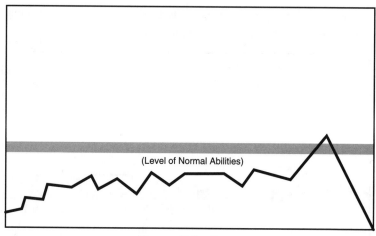

Figure 9-3   Pest

Pest vs. Underdog is a fairly even matchup, but again, audiences can easily become bored because the Pest, who functions as an irritant, often seems petty against a legitimate Underdog. Good examples of this matchup include *Home Alone* and *Bushwhacked.*

■ Strengthening Your Antagonist ■

Here are some techniques for making your antagonists more effective:

1. Make the Antagonist a Representative of "the World"

Just as the hero is strengthened by being separated from the world, the antagonist's power base comes from an alliance with that world, although the antagonist often takes those values to an extreme.

2. Establish the Antagonist's Strengths

It can be quite effective to give the antagonists at least one likable, even admirable, quality, because that prevents the audience from dismissing them at once as utter bad guys. These "seeds of greatness" can make the antagonist's eventual loss or defeat more provocative, and this is particularly true in the contest between adversaries and Everyman heroes, which can provide a forum for exploring issues of deeper emotional complexity.

3. Establish the Antagonist's Weakness

As with your hero, giving the antagonist an Achilles' heel can add excitement and unpredictability to the contest, especially when the antagonist is a Fiend.

Otherwise, it can seem implausible that heroes with lower levels of abilities would be able to win.

4. Establish Motives, Plans, and Goals

Often people feel that they are up against an unknown, or at least an unnamed, source of opposition, so it can be very effective to stagger revelations about the antagonist. One way is to reveal the antagonist's methods but not the motivation, as in *Die Hard*. Another possibility is to reveal the motive but not the identity for a while, as in the discovery of the bad cops in *Witness*. Either device can help create suspense and make ultimate revelations more effective. Additionally knowing an antagonist's goals and plans gives the audience a way to measure the character's success or failure at any point in the story. A clever and complex plan can also add to the audience's sense of the antagonist's power.

Secondary Characters

The function of *secondary characters* is to explain, examine, and heighten contrast between the hero and the world. Scenes with confidants, friends, lovers, supporters, mentors, and advisers allow a hero to express thoughts, desires, goals, plans, and values. They are characters used to define the hero and the hero's world. These characters are often the ones who really explain who the hero is and what drives him or her. Secondary characters can also be used to examine the world of the story including the antagonist's character, values, and world view, all of which intensifies the polarity between the hero and the world. The more you define one, the more you imply the conflict with the other. This also makes the hero more distinctive by contrast and makes the obstacles against the hero more formidable.

Secondary characters give depth, explanations, and richness to the main story. Often the plot is concerned with just the skeletal actions; secondary characters are a chance for the audience to learn the details.

For example, in *Escape from Alcatraz*, every scene, subplot, and secondary character that helps convey the hero's concern for humanity gives the audience a deep visceral sense of his values. Meanwhile, every scene of the hero's world, including the guards, the huge slamming steel doors, the hard stone halls, and the rigid regulations, conveys a sense of how inevitable the conflict is between the hero and the world.

Therefore, once you have chosen an arena for your story that amplifies the difference between the hero and the world, you need to populate both sides of that dramatic equation. You need to show the audience the people and events that explain and magnify the contrast of the two world views. Such divisions are an integral part of your dramatic equation, heightening the audience's sensitivity to the values and conflicts involved.

Important though they may be, make sure your secondary characters don't overshadow your hero and antagonist. This problem occurs frequently because secondary characters aren't the writer's alter egos (as the hero or antagonist is) and therefore seem easier to write.

Fleshing Out Characterizations

Characterization involves giving the audience all the pertinent information to assess the characters' strengths and weaknesses, and why they are so well suited to battle. The level of insight into your characters equals the emotional depth of your exploration into the human condition.

Some characters' emotional reactions to change are very complex—as Al Pacino's character in *Scent of a Woman*—but not all scripts need in-depth characters. Many high-concept films are marketable largely because audiences don't need to know a great deal about the characters' personalities in order to predict what kind of roller-coaster ride it's going to be. You don't need to know much about someone's personality to imagine the terror one feels being chased by an indestructible monster in *The Terminator*. The same is true in *Jurassic Park*. However, even mainstream commercial films like *Lethal Weapon* are strengthened by compelling characters. Meanwhile, soft-concept films like *Driving Miss Daisy, On Golden Pond, Il Postino, Mrs. Winterbourne,* or *Rambling Rose* will live or die on the strength of personalities.

1. Clarify the Character Arc

A *character arc* is the character's emotional reaction to the sequence of events that are your plot. For example, the plot of *Becoming Colette* details the husband's manipulations of his young wife. The changes she experiences, which take her from an innocent country girl to a renowned writer, are her emotional arc.

In order for character arcs to be successful, the audience must understand who the character is at the beginning of the story, who he or she is at the end, why each intervening change occurs, and why each one leads to the next. It also helps if the audience understands what forces are causing the change, what forces are making it difficult to deal with the change, and what the character's step-by-step reaction to each key moment is. One film that really excelled at this is *Mr. Holland's Opus.*

Some key moments for heroes or antagonists are the starting point, landmarks of change, the pivotal moment of change, and the end result. Character arcs can focus on in-depth emotional changes, or simply adjustments of problem-solving strategies. What is important is that there are increasing stages of difficulty and revealing reactions to those difficulties. That's what creates enough new information to keep your audience interested.

2. Focus Your Characterizations on the Present Tense

I often meet writers who put all their energy into figuring out the *back-story,* or personal history, of a character. They then spend a great deal of screen time on the resulting details, yet as the character proceeds throughout the story, it becomes clear that the details are irrelevant. They have not affected the character's actions or motives in any way.

Rather than providing back-story, focus your imagination on the actions, characteristics, language, and behavior that can make the character interesting in the current story. What determines whether a character is successful is how well that character evokes the audience's interest in the present tense. People develop strong, clear impressions about other humans based solely on present-tense body language, word choice, and general behavior without really knowing much about their back-stories at all.

Think about it. Don't you have firm impressions and opinions about your neighbors, coworkers, and many other people you pass in the course of the day even though you actually know little or nothing about their backgrounds? That's because the way someone speaks, moves, and looks gives you strong ideas of those people, and it is these qualities that are essential in establishing a characterization. The audience will only be curious about someone's back-story if there is something about their present-tense behavior that makes them curious.

3. Use Back-story Only If It's a Revelation

Writers should focus on the provocative and unique elements of a character's behavior in the present. Back-story is only valuable if it surprises the audience or explains why a person is acting in a curious manner. It's only interesting if it makes them act differently in the present or contradicts the audience's impressions of them, as in the revelations in *Hush, Hush Sweet Charlotte*.

The longer the audience holds an impression of the character, the more interesting such surprises will be. Therefore, it's a good idea to hold surprising revelations until later in the story. Startling revelations given to the audience an hour into a film, after the audience has developed its own expectation of the character, can be intriguing. Presenting that same information at the beginning will not have the same impact, because it doesn't contradict or enlighten the viewer's existing opinion. As a rule of thumb, don't use exposition unless it's going to significantly change the audience's opinion of the character.

4. Avoid Decorative Tags

Don't focus your creative energy only on coming up with imaginative eccentricities, or *decorative tags,* for characters unless they are somehow connected to deeper issues in the character or story. It is the information about characters' strengths and weaknesses that will prove pertinent to the central contest that is vital for the audience to know. It may be interesting to know that the character has some endearing trait, but unless the trait has some deeper meaning it will not increase the effectiveness of the story. Instead, what the audience must know about characters is how they will function in the matchup.

Decide on and convey the information that explains why the central matchup is exciting. Don't get attached to lots of details about your characters unless it affects the core dramatic questions of your story; focus on strengths and weaknesses of character that are pertinent to your central story.

5. What is the Character's Self-assessment? What is the World's Assessment? Is There a Gap?

Sometimes a hero thinks he is one thing and the audience thinks he is another. Some examples of this discrepancy are seen in *The Pink Panther, Black Sheep,* Felix in *The Odd Couple, Ace Ventura* and many of the characters created by Jim Carrey. These are heroes who think of themselves as Idols, while the audience perceives them as Underdogs. Fiends can think they are adversaries, or even think they are Idols.

Such miscalculations can be tragic or comic, but when they exist, it's important information for the audience to know. Other revealing information can be conveyed by how large the gap is between the two assessments. Why does the character have such a gap in their assessment? Usually there is a strong connection between the source of the gap and the central issues of the story.

6. Show, Don't Tell

Don't just *tell* the audience that the hero is likable or the antagonist is a Fiend. Make the audience *feel* that way. You must provoke the emotions in viewers so that they experience the power of your dramatic equation viscerally, and not just on a rational level. As we've discussed, the central secret of cinematic storytelling is that the story experience that matters is the one that happens inside viewers' negative space. Creating a sensation of loathing for the warden in *The Shawshank Redemption,* or enjoyment of Bruce Willis in *Die Hard* is essential for making the story come to life.

7. Don't Underestimate the Power of "Small Moments"

A *small moment* occurs when genuinely revealing data is disclosed but the character thinks the world isn't watching. In a small moment, the character makes no effort to put on a "mask," thereby allowing the audience to glimpse the "real" person. This is how the audience experiences their own lives, so seeing the characters' small moments help them bond to the heroes.

A great example of small moments was in *Dances with Wolves* when Kevin Costner's character was alone in the fort. If those moments had been edited out of the movie, the overall plot would not have changed, but the audience's sense of bonding to the character would have been significantly diminished. Not only would that have lessened the overall enjoyment of the film, but it could also have weakened the second half since the audience entered the Native Americans' foreign culture feeling very bonded with him. Without that closeness, the audience might have found it harder to relate to his acceptance of the tribe.

Small moments don't change the overall direction of the plot; however, they are absolutely crucial for creating a strong character bonding. The power of small moments comes from the fact that characters have let down their guard. Small moments give the audience more intimate knowledge of what the character is really like. More scripts fail due to lack of small moments than big moments. Small moments help the audience to bond to the characters; without that bonding the audience doesn't care about what happens to them.

Q U E S T I O N S

1. Is there an antagonist in your story?

2. If so, what kind of antagonist is best suited to your story?
   Fiend?
   Adversary?
   Pest?

3. What is the core opposition between the hero and his world?

4. What is the world's value system?
   What is the source of power?
   What type of logic dominates?

5. How is that opposition dramatized, presented, personalized?

6. Are you using your secondary characters to illuminate the values of either the hero or the world?

7. What are your hero's small moments?

8. How does your hero feel about himself?
   Where is the character's self-investment?
   What is the hero proud of?

9. What are the character's decorative tags?
   How do they connect with the central challenge?

10. Is your character interesting in the present tense and not just because of back-story?
    What is your character's main emotional arc?
    Is it central to your story, or secondary to a high concept conflict?

Momentum: Building Your Engine

Imagine that you've designed your roller coaster, built the pillars to support it, lured people into the cars, and then—nothing happens. No ride, no movement, nothing. That's what occurs when a roller coaster doesn't have an engine, and the same thing happens to an audience's interest if a story roller coaster doesn't propel them forward. Thus the next major element in building a story roller coaster is *momentum,* the energy that drives the audience's emotional and logical processes forward to completion.

Momentum is a crucial element in a successful story roller coaster, yet it is one of the least-addressed topics in screenwriting. When discussed at all, one theory claims that it's created by the hero's desire for a goal. However, there are many compelling films, like *The Graduate* and TV's *The Burning Bed,* in which heroes don't know what they want until far into the story, so what provides the momentum then? Another theory equates momentum with pacing, suggesting that a story will hold the audience's interest as long as actions, words, and images move quickly. However, speed is not enough to guarantee audience interest; for instance, several of my friends thought much of the second half of *Natural Born Killers* was agonizingly slow, despite the fact that events moved at lightning speed. The problem was they had no emotional or intellectual investment by that point in the story.

So what is momentum? Momentum is the audience's hunger to know what's going to happen next. That eagerness is not a passive state of mind, nor is it one that you can assume viewers will achieve by default. It's all too easy to "zone out" in front of the television or be distracted in a movie theater. When that happens, the audience's attention is on their negative space. What you want instead is for the positive space of your story to dominate their awareness. You want your audience totally absorbed in both an intellectual and emotional quest to find answers to questions that have formed in their minds. That fills their negative space with story information and intensifies their involvement in your story. That is the energy which creates the sensation of a compelling, fast-moving roller-coaster ride.

Asking and Answering Questions

As viewers process story information, questions spontaneously form in their negative space. Audience members ask themselves questions in order to get oriented, work their way through a myriad of information, and figure out what's important and what they think the information means. This is such an automatic process that it's virtually impossible to have the viewers not ask questions.

The first questions the audience usually ask are ones that help them get oriented in the story. During the first few minutes, their internal dialogue is often "Who is that guy?" "Is that his sister?" or "Why are they fighting?" Once a sense of orientation is established, questions then focus on the emotional and logical ramifications of plot changes, the importance of the change, or the characters' reaction to change.

The audience will not only have questions, but their minds will attempt to provide possible answers as well. Watch your own mental process next time you go to a film. After your questions begin, you will start to guess the answers. If the movie stopped halfway through and someone asked you to articulate your reasoning, you might be surprised to see just how thorough and detailed it was. That's because you've been evaluating the story material for possible clues, even if you weren't fully conscious of it.

Audiences not only try to guess the answers, but one of the reasons they stay with a story is to see if they are right. It's almost as though the story becomes a game in which they bet on the outcome and therefore have something at stake.

Audiences don't want their guesses to be completely right, of course. In fact, it's very disappointing if they are able to determine easily how a story's going to resolve. It makes them feel as though the game was not worth playing and that the storyteller let them down. On the other hand, they also don't want the final answers to be so obscure that the solution is impossible to find. That also makes the game seem like a waste of time, because there is no chance of winning.

What viewers want is something in the middle. When the solution is revealed, they want to realize that the story gave them enough clues to find the answer but the storyteller was clever enough to distract them from the clues' real significance. The resulting feeling is that they lost fairly, a very important criterion if the audience is to find a story emotionally satisfying.

Because of this constant question-and-answer process, every story is a mystery to viewers, regardless of its actual genre. Ideally, the audience should develop increasingly intense logical questions and emotional concerns that they are eager to have answered. It is that building intensity which creates the feeling of momentum. Making sure that viewers have enough information to get emotionally involved without making the story predictable demands very careful storytelling. This balance of giving viewers just the right amount of information is something that you shouldn't even worry about in first drafts. Early in the writing process, you need to focus on understanding what your dramatic center is, and how to best tell your story. But as you begin to polish your screenplay, you must pay close attention to the questions and answers that your story is provoking in viewers, because without creating a compelling "bread crumbs in the forest" dynamic, your story roller coaster will never develop strong momentum.

How Momentum Addresses Audience Needs

Momentum's primary function is to fulfill the audience's emotional need for *completion*. Every aspect of the intellectual and emotional energy employed in the question-and-answer process is the result of the audience's hunger for closure. Momentum can also address their hunger for *new information*. The very process of trying to find the answers to their internal questions forces the audience to constantly search through even seemingly familiar material for new meanings and insight. The audience's need for *conflict resolution* is addressed as they imagine various scenarios and evaluate whether each one will solve the issues in the story, and *bonding* occurs when they become totally absorbed in these efforts.

However, none of these needs can be successfully met if the screenplay fails to provide viewers with a strong sense of *author credibility*. The audience is continuously evaluating whether the effort to find answers is worthwhile. If the audience doubts that the storyteller will eventually answer their questions, they will withdraw from the process, killing momentum entirely. The audience will not commit themselves to playing the question/answer game if they don't think it's possible to win.

Creating Questions

One way to ensure author credibility is to make sure you intentionally plant the questions that you intend to answer in the audience's mind. Any question can create at least short-term interest, but it is very important that you consciously create questions that will focus the audience's attention on the aspects of the story that you want to dominate their negative space.

To create questions in the audience's mind you "black out" moments, deliberately omitting information that they need to fully understand the changes in your story. It's almost as though you line up all the scenes that will be necessary to tell your entire story, and then decide which ones you'll black out, thereby focusing the audience's attention on the conspicuously missing information.

An obvious example of blacked-out information occurred in the "Mission Impossible" TV series. In each episode the audience was allowed to see the portion of the scene in which team members were given their special tools and disguises, but they were not allowed to see the portion of the scene in which their use was explained. This led the audience to question how the devices would eventually be used, as well as to an exciting sense of discovery when the answers were eventually revealed.

Blacked-out information is central to creating a dynamic story. By omitting information, you intentionally focus the audience's interest on an event or piece of information, then leave it out. The audience will register an implied question in their negative space and begin looking for the answer, which contributes to the sense of momentum in your story.

Writers often think that the blacked-out information should create "yes or no" questions, but there are many limitations to constructing your central momentum around questions that have only two possible answers. At least fifty percent of your audience is bound to outguess you, and with Hollywood's obvious preference for happy endings, it's usually all too easy to anticipate the hero's success, or the villain's downfall.

However, there are two types of questions that are much harder to guess the answers to and thus are better at creating real doubt. They are "How?" and "Why?" These questions force viewers to get much more specific in their attempts to process the situation, creating stronger personalized involvement, and more hunger to know the outcome, which contributes to the sense of momentum.

Since the climax is the moment when the ultimate "How" or "Why" questions are answered, the decision about which type of story is best suited to your screenplay depends on your dramatic center and your dramatic equation. This is particularly true for the pivotal moment of change, which is when the audience should experience the dramatic center of your story and understand why the dramatic equation plays out as it does.

If your dramatic center has to do with motivations, feelings, or emotional realizations, you are probably telling a "Why" story. "Why" questions focus on the motive of a character or the logic of the plot progression. True life stories are often built around "Why" questions; the audience knows the criminal is guilty, but stays with the story to find out "Why." TV movies and miniseries often use "Why" questions to provide both immediate and long-term momentum, as in *Small Sacrifices* or *Deliberate Stranger,* the story of Ted Bundy.

"Why" stories take advantage of the audience's hunger for explanation. These stories often build towards revelation about motivation, thought process, or emotional priorities. In "Why" stories, the blacked-out scenes involve why the hero makes the decision. Psychological thrillers like *Silence of the Lambs* tend to be "Why" stories, as do most true-life crime stories. Many TV movies re-creating crimes leave the final reenactment to the end because that scene answers "Why". Some examples are *A Kiss Before Dying* and *Fatal Vision.*

"Who" questions seem like the driving force behind murder mysteries from *The Eiger Sanction* to *Miss Marple.* However, even stories that initially seem like "Who," such as *The Usual Suspects* and *Seven,* really are a variation of "Why" questions, since viewers won't be fully satisfied until they learn "Why" the guilty characters acted as they did.

Another way "Why" questions are important is the audience's tendency to ask "Why now". This usually occurs in viewers' minds when something in the plot progression or character's emotional arc doesn't seem credible. This jolting sensation can separate the audience from the story, at least momentarily, so if the question isn't convincingly answered sometime later, it hurts author credibility. On the other hand, if the jolt has been intentionally created for emphasis and the answer is supplied later, as occurs in *The World According to Garp* when the main character's son is killed in a car accident, it can be a very effective way to bring special attention to an aspect of the story.

If your fascination is with the practical, problem-solving techniques and rational judgments, your story is probably a "How." "How" questions focus on the process of emotional or logical problem solving, and the essential question is "How will that intention get accomplished?" Examples would be "How will they get back into Alcatraz?" in *The Rock,* or "How will the villains pull off their hijacking of a subway car?" in *The Taking of Pelham One-Two-Three.*

"How" stories involve the central question of how the hero will win. Rather than focusing the audience on easily predictable questions such as *whether* the hero will win, "How" stories center suspense on *how* the hero will achieve the goal. "How" stories are particularly useful with Idol heroes, such as Dirty Harry, Perry Mason, Superman, or Columbo, since there's not strong suspense about whether the Idol hero will succeed. However, if you leave in the scenes where the problems become evident and black out the scenes which convey the hero's strategy, then the question "How will the hero win?" can be quite compelling.

The decision to focus a cinematic story on "How" or "Why" questions usually occurs in later drafts once writers fully understand the dramatic center of their story and realize which questions will best focus the audience's attention on the central dynamics of the story. Also, a story doesn't have to be fully a "Why" or "How" story. In fact, often a "Why" main plot will be balanced by "How" subplots or vice versa. In such stories, the "How" element addresses the external actions of the plot, while the "Why" element addresses character motivation.

As the writer creates a trail of "How" or "Why" questions for the audience to follow, the audience develops an increasing need to know the ultimate answers, which provides a sense of satisfaction when they are finally revealed. If you create momentum by focusing the audience's attention on the important issues, you will intensify the key dynamics of your story, because what viewers think about in their negative space will dominate their experience with your story.

Curiosity and Suspense

There are two states of mind that can be created by intentionally provoking questions in the audience's mind. They are curiosity and suspense. Both are valuable for creating and sustaining audience interest and forward momentum.

Take sports, for example. If people watching a football game only know the most basic rules, they will probably lose interest quickly because even though they know what's happening, they don't understand its significance. In contrast, if they know all the rules, have extensive knowledge of the teams, believe the teams are evenly matched, and have a strong preference as to which team will win, they will watch the same game with a passionate level of interest because they understand the significance of the possible outcomes. They just don't know which will occur.

Curiosity is equivalent to the lower level of interest in the football game. It occurs when viewers know what events are happening, but they don't know why. Curiosity is easy to create, because all that is needed is a discrepancy between the events in a story and the audience's sense of the norm. Such norms are created by everyday life events or expectations generated by previously established story information. For example, if a character were established as easy-going and good-natured then suddenly began a tirade for no apparent reason, curiosity would be created by a story-based discrepancy. By the same token, if an ordinary-looking woman suddenly shrieks after seeing a red hat on the ground in the first scene of a script, the audience would also recognize the discrepancy, based on their real-life experiences.

If you want to create curiosity, you give the audience full information about the immediate events, but you black out the explanation. For example, in the opening sequence of the film *Shoot to Kill*, the audience sees a pajama-clad man frantically using keys to open the thick glass door of a commercial establishment. Moments later he is in a jewelry store, where he hurriedly throws diamonds into a container, carelessly dropping many on the floor. Within seconds, the audience is curious: What's going on here? The normal expectation is that burglars are much more deliberate and not dressed in pajamas, so the viewers' minds immediately start piecing together the available information hoping to discover an explanation that makes sense.

Because curiosity can be created so quickly, it is very useful in overcoming resistance at the beginning of the story. Curiosity engages the audience because they begin forming questions in their negative space. Once viewers sense a discrepancy, questions automatically spring to their mind, thrusting their interest forward, which creates momentum. But since curiosity is based on an active sense of disorientation, the audience can soon become uncomfortable with their lack of knowledge, and that sense of discomfort increases over time. Eventually that conscious dissatisfaction nags at them in their negative space and therefore hurts their sense of momentum. So once you plant curiosity in the viewers' minds, you need to understand that the "meter is running." You must give them an answer or some hint that you will eventually answer their question or you risk hurting your author credibility and distracting them from the story.

A better storytelling technique is to provoke initial curiosity, then build on that interest by turning it into suspense. Suspense is similar to the second level of interest in our football analogy. It occurs when the audience understands the significance of possible outcomes, but doesn't know which one will occur.

To create suspense, you must give the audience all necessary information about the possible ramifications of outcomes, but black out the knowledge of which one will occur. Using the *Shoot to Kill* example, the suspense begins once the audience understands that the man is the owner of a swank jewelry store and his wife has been kidnapped. His carelessness is due to his frantic distress in trying to comply with the ransom demands. What they don't know now is if he will succeed.

Suspense is most successful when the audience also has developed an emotional bond with the characters, and because suspense is based on a stronger level of audience orientation than curiosity, it can be maintained for longer stretches of time. However, due to the audience's emotional involvement and conscious concern for the characters, an active sense of suspense can become increasingly unpleasant for viewers. One of the reasons suspense generates strong momentum is that the audience eagerly searches for an answer in order to bring the unpleasant sensation to an end. If suspense goes on too long without any promise of relief, viewers will begin to resist the continued unpleasantness, disrupting their concentration and working against the momentum you want to build.

A film doesn't have to be a thriller or a horror film to use suspense. In fact, virtually every successful story provokes that sensation because it is the natural result of viewers' eagerness to guess what will happen next and get the answers to their questions. This state of expectation can't occur until viewers are given enough information to make some assessment of the situation. Creating expectation in your audience requires you to provoke a sense of direction, doubt, and desire within their negative space.

Direction

The first thing an audience needs in order to develop expectations is a sense of *direction* about where the story is going.

In order to feel a basic sense of direction, viewers must have some idea of who the main characters are, what the hero wants to achieve, what the obstacles are, what kind of matchup exists between the hero and the challenge, what is at stake, and at least some indication of how they are supposed to feel about the story. The audience doesn't need to know all of this immediately, but they do need a sense that the storyteller knows and is prepared to let them in on it at some point.

The need for direction is particularly strong in the beginning of the story, because the audience cannot assess whether later information is pertinent until they have a sense of what the story is about. The sense of direction is usually established in the form of a story "click," which is when the audience gets an initial sense of what kind of story it's going to be. It is the "Oh, I get it" moment that usually occurs when the audience understands that the hero's encounter with change has begun. For example, in *Chinatown*, the story click is when Jack Nicholson encounters Faye Dunaway and learns that he has been tricked into taking the case. In *The Verdict*, it is the moment when Paul Newman rejects the settlement and decides to take the case to court.

Some writers think of the story click as the "inciting incident." However, that label focuses your attention on the internal logic of a story, while the real importance of a story click is as the key moment of orientation for the audience. The quicker the audience is given enough information to assess the starting point, the more clearly they can process the significance of the changes in the story.

This does not have to be done in the first ten pages, as conventional wisdom suggests, but you should be conscious of the fact that the audience will not totally relax until they have this information. They won't feel comfortable until they have some sense of direction because they don't know where to focus their attention or what criteria to use to process and evaluate the ongoing story information.

Many writers are reluctant to give viewers too much information because they are concerned that the audience will become bored. Ironically, it is the lack of direction that is alienating to viewers. So don't be too subtle in your presentation of the story click, because viewers are actively looking for that sense of "you are here" on the map of the story to give them a basic sense of orientation.

Another way to give an audience a sense of direction without telling them too much is by using setups and payoffs. A *setup* is a nugget of story information that will answer the audience's questions later on. Setups hint at what people, events, and issues will be central to the story, thus giving the audience a sense of direction, but all the relevant information is not revealed at that time. Instead, setups are a promise that the author makes to the viewers, and the *payoff* is the moment when that promise is fulfilled. As more setups occur, the trail of nuggets gradually leads viewers through your story, creating momentum which intensifies as the clues accumulate and viewers become increasingly eager to see their significance.

There are two kinds of setups. *Foreshadowing* is a conspicuous setup, an intentionally theatrical hint that viewers should pay attention to some piece of story information. An example of foreshadowing is the use of music that signals the presence of the shark in *Jaws*, or a closeup of a knife which is later revealed to be the murder weapon. The other kind of setup is *planted seeds*, which are inconspicuous setups. This kind of setup is not obvious when first introduced but proves to contain useful information later in the story. In fact, part of creating a fun roller-coaster ride for viewers is the sensation created when planted seeds later provide unexpected answers to key questions the audience has been asking.

The writer's challenge in using planted seeds setups is to distract viewers from their real importance by focusing the characters' attention, and therefore the audience's, on some secondary concern. In fact, the sense of direction created for the audience by planted seed setups does not come from their eventual revelations, but from the disguise writers use to conceal their real significance when they are first introduced.

Planting seeds can be a very effective storytelling technique and enhances author credibility when done well. In order that it be done well, you have to make sure that the viewers think they fully understand the significance of the planted seed at the outset and don't realize they've been duped until the additional layer of meaning is revealed. For example, in *The Big Easy*, Ellen Barkin makes love with Dennis Quaid, then comes downstairs the next morning and pats him on the rear only to discover that it's his brother she patted. The focus of that scene is her embarrassment as she quickly leaves the apartment, and the audience's attention is on how passionate, yet tenuous, the relationship between the lovers really is. However, a half hour later in the story, when the brother is shot on the street because he looks like Dennis Quaid, the audience suddenly understands the real significance of the earlier scene.

When used successfully, planted seeds add excitement to the roller-coaster ride, because the audience experiences such moments as a "gotcha!" in films like *Malice*. Such revelations also suggest that viewers should stay on their toes because there could be more surprises along the way. There are a lot of levels on which a story can be satisfying for the audience, but the ability to pick up the necessary clues and then use them later on is a big part of it. In a well-scripted film like *No Way Out*, some of the definite thrill in the final portion of the movie is the fact that all the information we have gathered about the character and the situation comes into play.

The sensation that the audience experiences when setups work well, whether they are foreshadowed or planted seeds, is that the nugget of information viewers picked up eventually comes in handy, so they feel clever to have noticed it before and smart to understand how it answers their current questions. However, the desire for that sensation explains why unanswered setups are so frustrating for viewers.

Cumulatively these promises add up and linger in the audience's mind. That's why you want to make sure that you set up everything you pay off, and vice versa. The failure to provide payoffs prevents viewers from having that sense of completion and satisfaction for which they turn to stories.

Here are some general tips on creating a sense of direction:

1. Only Set Up What is Absolutely Necessary

Because the audience often puts a great deal of energy into picking up all available clues, you should only set up what is absolutely necessary. Otherwise, information that you only mean as "atmospheric" can be taken by the audience as a significant clue, temporarily giving them the wrong impression or even taking them significantly off course when processing your story.

2. The More Conspicuously Something is Set Up, the Bigger the Payoff Must Be

The longer you taunt viewers with foreshadowing, or hide a secret from them in conspicuous ways, the more important the ultimate answer becomes and the more impact it must have when it's revealed. If this doesn't happen the audience will feel a sense of disappointment and the anti-climatic moment will create an unintentional dip in their roller-coaster experience.

In the movie *The Outlaw Josey Wales,* Clint Eastwood spit repeatedly. It was such a prominent part of his character that it seemed to be leading to a major payoff, like winning a crucial shootout because he spit in his opponent's eye. When the payoff came only halfway through the movie and was played only for a minor bit of comic relief, the resulting disappointment caused the story roller coaster to momentarily falter.

3. Don't Answer Questions Until the Audience "Asks"

Don't give the audience key information until you have created curiosity about it in their negative space. For example, if you want to tell your characters' back-story, make sure that you've created some genuine curiosity about their past. Before that, even the most interesting information will feel like unnecessary exposition or distracting details. Additionally, because the audience doesn't have a context for that information, its importance could easily be lost. In contrast, learning the same information after the audience has developed questions becomes an exciting revelation, which is part of the fun of a great roller-coaster ride.

Slowing the momentum of a story for information which doesn't answer the audience's questions often causes a break in the forward thrust and can even bring the audience's roller coaster to a halt. That's why many people don't like flashbacks. There's no hard-and-fast rule that says not to use them, but as with any exposition, use them sparingly and only to answer questions already established in the audience's negative space.

You can also disguise exposition by incorporating it within a bigger emotional moment. Information revealed during a fight or as comic relief can be readily absorbed by the audience. Much like planted seeds, the secret is to focus your characters' attention in the scene on something rather than the exposition.

4. Reveal Information Gradually Rather Than Explaining It All At Once

It's more effective to reveal answers gradually, or to reveal only portions of answers until the cumulative pattern all makes sense, than to have long, expository scenes. Even when they are well done, as with the wife's confession in *Presumed Innocent,* to say nothing of the cliché final scene in which the detective brings the suspects together to reveal the killer, such explanations tend to answer the audience's logical questions rather than viewers' emotional concerns.

The gradual revelations, as in *Hush, Hush Sweet Charlotte,* can really help build pillar height, especially if they are slowly exposing answers to the central questions that drive the story. They also let viewers know that you are in control, and that they can sit back and trust that they will get all their questions answered eventually.

5. Don't Give the Audience "Small Print" While They're Still Looking for "Headlines"

An example of "headlines" vs. "small print" is the first scene in *The Big Easy.* While the audience is trying to get their initial orientation, or "*headlines,*" such as "Is Dennis Quaid a cop?" and "Is that body dead?", the characters suddenly launched into a "small print" detailed discussion of possible killers and complicated motives.

The problem is that in explaining so much about the bad guys who had never even appeared on screen, the audience had no sense of orientation in which to process the details.

6. There is a Ratio Between How Important Information Is and How Quickly It Is Paid Off

If a setup provokes an important question about story information that significantly changes the status quo, the audience needs some time to adjust to the new possibilities before the status quo is changed again. Thus the ratio between the importance of the setup and the interval of its payoff is crucial. If the interval is either too short or too long, the emotional impact of the cause and effect is lessened. Too long an interval can force a story roller coaster to lose its forward momentum, while intervals that are too brief can make the story seem melodramatic.

7. Pay Off Everything You Set Up and Vice Versa

Because of the effort an audience puts into processing conspicuous setups and looking for rewarding payoffs, disappointing viewers at either end of that process can significantly undercut the story's ultimate impact. Unresolved setups or "loose ends" are very dissatisfying, while payoffs which are not well justified and integrated into the story's central construction feel as though the writer is cheating the viewers, resulting in a major loss of author credibility.

Doubt

Another important element in developing momentum is generating *doubt* in the audience's mind about whether the hero can overcome the obstacles. Creating genuine doubt can be very difficult since today's cinematically literate audience is well aware that most Hollywood movies have happy endings.

One technique, which we've already discussed, is centering your story around "Why" or "How" questions, which are much less predictable than "Will the hero succeed, yes or no?" You can also use plot twists, unpredictable personality changes and events, and intense separations between the hero and the world to imply an inevitable sense of conflict and overwhelming odds.

Another technique is to focus viewers' attention on what an exciting and well-suited matchup there is between the hero and the antagonist, or whatever kind of obstacle is central to the story. Because most writers instinctively give plenty of screen time to the story's hero, it's important to make sure you spend enough screen time showing viewers how powerful the obstacles are. Whether its the unpredictability of nature, as in *Twister,* the determination of the antagonists, as in *Die Hard,* or the size of the conspiracy against the hero, as in *Three Days of the Condor,* the more the audience knows about the opponents' power, the more genuine doubt can be created about the ultimate outcome.

Desire

The last crucial ingredient to create momentum is desire, an *emotional need* to see the hero succeed, learn what finally happens, or discover the pivotal moment of change and what that implies about the dramatic equation.

Ensuring that the audience develops an emotional need to stay with the story is why creating rooting interest for the hero is so important. If the story fulfills all three criteria for real rooting interest—that the hero is capable of winning, deserving to win, and strengthened through the conflict—the result is an intensified emotional and logical investment in the hero's victory.

There are several things that audiences can find deeply satisfying. One is to see heroes triumph over change and find a way to deal with the new status quo appropriately. Another is to see heroes get away with whatever risks they took as they fought to achieve their goals. That may mean that the heroes don't have to pay a price for breaking the rules, or that the price they pay seems worth it. Viewers can even find satisfaction when the hero doesn't succeed in the eyes of the world as long as the hero feels the sacrifice is worthwhile, as in films like *Serpico*. Often this sense of peace occurs because the heroes believe the world is better off because of their sacrifices, or they know they did the best they could.

Viewers also desire to have their story questions answered. Audiences want to "make life make sense," to have their questions answered, and to see if their guesses were right. That hunger for completion is a primal desire, and audiences will lose enthusiasm for the story if they don't believe they will eventually receive the answers to their questions. The audience is looking for the story's final resolution. It is the end result of your dramatic equation and must be true to both the logical and emotional questions of your story. The logic for the happy ending or unhappy ending needs to be set up within the story. A contrived happy ending is not satisfying because it is not well justified and does not give the audience the sense of "fair play" that they desire.

In a well-constructed story, there will be surprises along the way, but by the time the ending is revealed, there should be a sense of inevitability. It is possible to simply end the story with ambivalence, but you need to be aware that you are working against the audience's innate hunger for resolution, and so you must find some other way to provide a satisfying sense of closure.

All these seemingly different desires actually play into a deeper, more profound hunger to know the answer to the dramatic equation. In that sense, the entire story becomes one big question, and the answer (the outcome which completes the story's statement) is climactic because it allows the audience to experience the emotional power of your dramatic center as well as the logical satisfaction of the plot. A large part of your audience's satisfaction depends on whether the dramatic equation is genuinely expressed by the totality of your story.

Finally, the sense of *denouement,* or the slowing of momentum, occurs most successfully when the audience's desire to know has been sated, allowing them to begin an emotional tapering-off period. It's a good idea to keep the final denouement as short as possible, because with no more questions driving their interest forward, audiences often feel restless if it goes on too long. All they really need is a little screen time to regain their composure, to come back up to the real world without getting the emotional "bends."

Now that we understand how a story's forward momentum affects the audience's emotional reaction, let's examine the importance of style, which intensifies the emotional impact of your story dynamics.

Q U E S T I O N S

1. What do you want the audience to wonder about?

2. How does that connect to the dramatic center of your story?

3. How does it affect the dramatic equation of your story?

4. Is it a "How" or a "Why" story?
   What are the central "How" or "Why" questions?
   Does it advance the heroes' inner motivation?
   Outer goal?
   Are there subplots that answer the other questions?

5. Is anything set up?
   Foreshadowed or planted seeds?

6. Is everything that is set up paid off?

7. When do you use curiosity?
   Suspense?

8. How do you provide direction for viewers?
   Provoke doubt?
   Ensure desire?

9. Have you created a sense of direction for your audience?
   How?

10. Have you created a sense of genuine doubt?
    How?

11. Have you created an exciting matchup?
    How?

12. Have you created strong desire in your audience for your hero to win?
    How?

Style: Greasing the Tracks

Now your roller coaster is built, people are on board, and the engine is ready to go. However, to make sure your roller coaster provides the compelling ride it was designed to deliver, you must make sure that every inch of your track is as polished as possible. Otherwise, the disruption created by jolts and halts and snags and jerks can weaken the appeal of even the best-designed ride.

Thus the last major element in building a story roller coaster is *style*, the imaginative restatement of the major dynamics of your story integrated into every layer of the script. It should be evident in the plot, characters, momentum devices, visual effects, narrative techniques, and any other component you use to tell your story.

"Style is the feather in the arrow, not the feather in the cap," a great quote by George Sampson of Cambridge University, really says it all, because style, if well used, helps your script soar and can give it intensity, unity, and focus. The peripheral messages conveyed by the constant and consistent use of style do not contribute just to the audience's logical understanding of the story, but to their visceral understanding of the dramatic equation as well, leading them to experience the dramatic center.

Style works as an intensifier so that viewers can experience the world of the story in a more subjective and intense way. It can help magnify the separation between the hero and the world. It helps create an all-enveloping sensory experience that heightens the audience's reaction, sending them the key signals of your story on both the conscious and subconscious levels.

In order for your story to be the most effective, you must take viewers beyond their conscious assessment of your story. Yet the process of presenting story information is not always evocative enough to create emotional resonance, especially when your story is still on the page.

That's why style can be so effective. The very peripheral nature of the associations viewers make in their negative space to stylistic choices makes it powerful. It appeals to the audience on a deep, nonverbal level. By surrounding viewers with color, rhythms, language, movement, settings, and sounds, all of which combine to create a unified visceral sensation, you can reach them in a primal, non-intellectualized way.

When successfully used, it will also help suggest images to executives, directors, and producers that are vivid and evocative, making it easier for them to "see" a script in their minds, helping to convince them that it will make a great film.

Audiences go to films for an experience, for sensation. They want to feel sated, inundated, which is why films that generate strong emotional impact are usually big hits. It is usually style, carefully orchestrated to intensify the logical and emotional elements of the story, that contributes most to impact.

How Does It Feel . . . ?

Stories are most effective when they answer the audience's hunger to know *"How does it feel to . . . ?"* and style is the most effective way to transcend a one-dimensional, intellectualized appreciation and create an all-enveloping sensual experience to answer that question in a visceral and immediate way. "How does it feel to die of cancer?" "How does it feel to win the lottery?" "How does it feel to climb Mt. Fuji?" are variations of the essential desire audiences go to films to fulfill.

That's because an effective answer to "How does it feel to . . . ?" addresses all four of the audience's primal needs at once. It addresses the need for *new information* by answering their curiosity about "How does it feel to . . . " be an astronaut or sail around the world—without having to take the risks. When this kind of story is effective, it is one of the most thrilling sensations, a way to experience how other people's lives feel, to see how other people live, and experience a new point of view.

The audience *bonds* with the story and the characters, because style helps viewers imagine the world of the characters and to see it through their eyes. In fact, the more subjectively that information and sensations can be conveyed to viewers, the more immediate an impact they will have, and it's the peripheral, emotion-based style choices that enhance the sense of subjectivity. In answering

"How does it feel to . . . ?," you don't just tell us how the character feels, but ideally you make the audience feel it as well.

A good example of this was evident in *Ghost.* The moment Patrick Swayze was shot, there was a flurry of quick cuts, startling images, and shocking juxtapositions. For a moment, viewers didn't know what was happening, which was exactly the sensation the character was also experiencing. As a result, the film didn't just tell viewers he was scared and disoriented, it made the audience *feel* it the same way.

Conflict resolution also ties into "How does it feel to . . . ?" You can intensify the audience's understanding of the hero's fear of change, the power of the opposition, and the matchup between the hero and the obstacle course through creative style choices. A good example is *Throw Mama from the Train,* in which the physical attributes of the actress who played the mother, the use of extreme closeups, and other subjective intensifiers really made the audience understand both Danny DeVito's and Billy Crystal's dilemma.

"How does it feel to . . . ?" also addresses the need for *completion* because style helps provide an all-enveloping sensation of thorough satiation.

Remember, every choice you make in your screenplay will either enhance or detract from your audience's ability to become absorbed in your story's positive space. If the audience's awareness of the negative space can recede, they will experience the story roller coaster with full richness and satisfaction.

■ How Does This Apply to Writers? ■

At this point in my class, I am usually asked, "Isn't the style of a film the domain of the director?" The answer is yes, to some extent it is. By the time an audience sees a *completed* film they are seeing the results of the other artists' choices made while transferring the story from page to screen.

However, there is a great deal you can do while the story is still on the page to convey tone, pacing, colors, textures, rhythm, attitude, humor, irony, and many other stylistic choices which signal to the reader a vivid impression of the story you are creating.

As a result of its peripheral powers, style is a potent tool, and one that conveys individuality and vision faster than any other. It is an opportunity to make a personal statement. Style can charm, shock, amuse, seduce, intrigue, or startle viewers, all of which can help overcome viewers' initial resistance to a story and provide strong moment-to-moment interest, as well as intensify the major dynamics of your story.

Your unique "voice" is comprised of all the stylistic choices that you make. Yet so few writers use style consciously and consistently that using it well is certain to help your script stand out from the crowd. So don't abdicate in this vital area. Make active and consistent choices and incorporate them into your screenplay to bring your story to life and express your unique voice.

Style as Signature

Think of Quentin Tarantino, who shocked and seduced the entertainment industry with *Pulp Fiction,* Harold Pinter's streamlined dialogue, Shane Black's action stories like *The Last Boy Scout,* Horton Foote's emotionally powerful scripts like *Places In the Heart,* Joe Eszterhas' titillating stories like *Basic Instinct,* or John Patrick Shanley's delightful sense of human foibles in *Moonstruck.* The first thing that comes to mind is their style, which is immediately apparent on the page. You don't need to see the completed films to feel their distinctive voices. In fact, often a screenwriter isn't really considered a success *until* the world can see a recognizable style. Oliver Stone was a journeyman writer and director making a living in the field long before he became prominent. It wasn't until the audience began to see a recognizable signature to his work that he really developed into a major presence in the field.

■ The Two Basic Tools of Style ■

Despite all the millions of distinct and fascinating cinematic stories which can be made, there are actually only two tools that filmmakers—and therefore screenwriters—have at their command; *sight* and *sound.* Everything writers want to convey about their worlds has to be "made" out of either something the audience can see or something they can hear.

However, through the imaginative use of stylistic elements, you can create such a rich sense of atmosphere that people can feel almost as though they are experiencing the events with all five senses. In fact, the challenge for the writer is to use visual and auditory clues to go beyond those two senses and suggest images that appeal to the other senses.

1. The Visual

We have all heard that "films are a visual medium," but why is that true? The reason is that sight dominates humans' sensory input. Eighty percent of all information about the world around us comes through the eyes. As a result, the communication between the process of visual input and translating that information into meaningful data is finely tuned, and the brain is able to process the information easily.

As a result, visual stylistic choices conveyed in clear, concise stage directions can quickly create provocative images in the audience's mind. Their emotions often react instantaneously, allowing your screenplay to take on a vitality and immediacy that significantly heightens its impact. Your choice of colors, props, actions, gestures, shapes, textures, movement, characters' physical appearance and mannerisms, sets, costumes, actors' appearances, and locations can all convey visual information to readers, even on the printed page. *Batman, Howard's End,* "Miami Vice," *Interview with a Vampire,* or *Blade Runner* are all examples of films or shows that have a strong visual component.

2. The Auditory

People get only twenty percent of their information from their ears. Yet sound is a potent source of emotion often overlooked, especially at the script phase.

Sound gets much of its potency from the fact that it can harness people's emotional energy in the very process of trying to understand the location and significance of the source. Until all of those factors are processed, there is an undercurrent of fear because the required gap of time needed to understand auditory information leaves humans temporarily vulnerable.

To completely understand its power, try watching a horror film with no sound, then listening to the soundtrack of a horror film without the visuals, and see which one is scarier. However, sound does not have to produce just fear. It can add strong atmosphere, texture, and tension—think of the ticking clock on the mantel, the sirens racing by on the way to a fire, lovers trying to have an intimate discussion on a crowded subway platform. There are many sound applications in film: dialogue, sound effects, silence, volume, frequency, music. It is really limited only by your imagination.

Style Spectrum

Now that you are aware of the tools available to you, the next decision to make is how intense and conspicuous you want to be in the use of style. Some stylistic choices are very obvious; others are more subtle. How glaring or subtle you are in your stylistic choices will determine where your screenplay falls on the style spectrum.

1. Transparent Style

This kind of style choice is in the middle of the style spectrum and contains nothing conspicuous. It seems to be a realistic portrayal of the world of the film. Transparent style seems invisible because it doesn't call attention to itself. But transparent does not mean nonexistent.

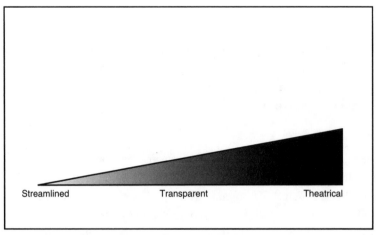

Streamlined   Transparent   Theatrical

Figure 11-1   Style Spectrum

In reality there is no such thing as a lack of style, even if there seems to be abdication of it. The writer may well be making subtle choices about colors, styles, and textures that seem so appropriate to the story that they are virtually unnoticeable.

Some examples of effective use of transparent style are *Ransom, All the President's Men, Tootsie, Howard's End, Up Close and Personal,* and *The Brothers McMullen.*

2. Theatrical Style

One extreme of the spectrum is used when recognizable factors of the world we know are evident, then exaggerated. *Blade Runner,* for example, seemed to be a statement of technology gone mad.

Use of this type of high-profile style loses its effectiveness if it becomes unfocused or too cluttered. In my opinion, *The Adventures of Baron Münchhausen* marked such an occurrence. Certainly that was an amazing-looking film and virtually each clip of celluloid was an event, but because it lacked a recognizable truth at the center, I had to get reoriented time and time again, and my dominant impression of the film was a wild visual ride with no emotional center. I'm not saying there wasn't any; Terry Gilliam is a brilliant filmmaker with a very sophisticated view of the world, but I couldn't "get it."

Some examples of effective use of theatrical style are *Batman; Earth Girls are Easy; Strictly Ballroom; Jeffrey; Brazil; Blade Runner; The Addams Family; Spy Hard; The Adventures of Priscilla, Queen of the Desert;* and *Mars Attacks!*

3. Streamlined Style

The other extreme on the spectrum represents style used sparingly. The effectiveness of *streamlined* style depends on choosing just the right "revealing details," because through those you will reveal the meaning of your story. Streamlined style often reminds me of my days in "experimental theater." We hung black drapes at the back of the stage, and all the actors wore black leotards. Then the cowboy wore cowboy boots, the ballerina wore a tutu, etc.

This type of style choice gives emphasis by eliminating clutter and everyday objects, so that the colors or objects left on the screen have added impact. If you make this style choice, it's very important that you get clarity on what aspects of your story must be emphasized and which can be made secondary. In *Dick Tracy,* the emphasis was on the color scheme, but all other visual elements had simple lines and few distracting details. Often this style tends to be more serious. Many foreign films fall into this category. Other examples of streamlined style include *Closet Land, Interiors, Twelve Angry Men, Our Town, Death and the Maiden, Fargo, Edward II, The Crow,* and "The Honeymooners."

■ Areas of Style Choices ■

In addition to the intensity and conspicuous nature of your style choices, you have a variety of categories in which you can make interesting style choices.

1. Color

The *color palette* of a picture conveys a real sense of time and place, even if just mentioned occasionally in stage directions. Think of how the cold, gray world of *The Addams Family,* the electric hues of *Clueless,* or the bleak colors of *The Crow* conveyed both the atmosphere and a sense of the films' dramatic center. Color was also used effectively in *The Wizard of Oz* and *Schindler's List,* which contrasted black-and-white with color.

Granted, you cannot capture completely the full intensity of these stylistic choices on the printed page, but carefully chosen details about color can plant the right kinds of images in the readers' minds.

2. Texture

You can also convey a strong sense of texture that enriches the reader's experience of your script. For example, texture played a big part in conveying the dramatic contrast of the two worlds in *Someone to Watch Over Me,* or in *The Brady Bunch Movie.* Texture is the "adjective" describing your scripts, as in the steamy sensibility of *Body Heat,* the gritty world of *Midnight Cowboy,* the lush tropical world of *Congo,* and the oddly sterile fantasy universe of *Edward Scissorhands* or *The Hudsucker Proxy.* Texture is also evident in the different images, sophistication of language, and motives that distinguish more primitive horror films like Wes Craven's *Nightmare on Elm Street* from Clive Barker's *Hellraiser.*

3. Rhythm

Rhythm is a very potent area of choice because it is the metronome of the story. Rhythm can be conveyed in dialogue, length of scenes, or speed of events. It can be constant within a script, as in *Bringing Up Baby,* or it can be used to create bold contrasts which juxtapose slow, quiet scenes with fast-paced action sequences.

For example, a film like *Barry Lyndon* makes brilliant use of slowness. Stanley Kubrick captures the very essence of life in that pre-Industrial time with the dramatically measured pacing that is incorporated into every aspect of the film. The dialogue is long and formal, the costumes heavy, the camera angles just right. It would be possible to cut that film down to a more conventional rhythm by simply editing out the long crosses and slow scenes, but it would change the film fundamentally. In contrast, the film *His Girl Friday,* the raucous comedy with Cary Grant and Rosalind Russell, captured the vibrancy of the characters, the newspaper business, and one-upmanship of the central relationship by its split-second pacing, overlapping dialogue, and quick, short scenes. The TV series "Moonlighting," and the film *One Fine Day* also attempted to create the same energy.

Of course, your entire story doesn't have to be set at one pace. In fact, it is often extremely effective to increase speed to intensify action sequences as the final events of the story play out or slow the pace to make suspense almost unbearable. Other choices will make an important scene linger on the screen, either by elongating it or by playing a key moment in slow motion. Try to use rhythm consciously, enhancing each twist and turn of your roller coaster.

4. Duration

Duration is another interesting category of style. How much screentime you take for events to occur in your story, in fact, how long a story you decide to write, and how much time you give readers to adjust to one significant change before the next occurs can make a significant difference in its emotional impact on the reader.

Take Ken Burns' brilliant *Civil War*. The very pace at which the story unfolded, the actual screen time the audience spent with various characters, helped bring the events alive. At first the thirteen-hour film may have seemed slow and even a touch repetitive. Yet by the last night, when viewers finally learned what happened to the people with whom they'd spent so much time, viewers were deeply and even unexpectedly moved. The same is true of a well-structured miniseries like "Roots," or epic films like *War and Peace* or *Gone with the Wind*. Even daytime dramas gain much of their emotional impact simply because of the number of hours viewers spend with them.

Most people reading this book probably aren't interested in writing such long cinematic events. But even in stories that last two hours or less, how you apportion your screentime, how many plot events you include, and how much time you give readers to adjust to each significant change will affect how your readers experience the story.

5. Scale

Some examples of movies that use big scale are *Superman, The Hunt for Red October, Jurassic Park,* and *Independence Day.* The vistas are sweeping, the issues affect the entire world, and the impending change is on a grand scale.

In contrast, films on a smaller scale are the more intimate stories of *The Accidental Tourist, Remains of the Day, Carrington,* or *Madame Butterfly.* Those are personal stories, often set in confined spaces, about seemingly small moments of change that actually change the characters' lives forever.

6. Proportion

Understanding and using proportion, the contrast between large and small, can also convey powerful story dynamics to your readers.

Honey, I Shrunk the Kids and Eddy Murphy's *The Nutty Professor* had a field day playing with the concept of disproportionate physical objects. The original *Unfaithfully Yours,* by comedy genius Preston Sturgess, was about a jealous husband who assumes the perfect murder of his wife will only take a small amount of effort, yet in reality becomes a gigantic mess.

7. Physical Proximity

The *physical distance* between the viewers and the objects can also be used to enhance their emotional impact. In general the further away from the norm things are, either extremely close or extremely far, the more reaction it will provoke from viewers.

For example, in *A Clockwork Orange,* there is a closeup of an eyelid being pried open, which gives added visceral impact to the moment. In contrast, the distance between the viewers and the photographed lovers in *Blow Up* adds mystery and suspense; a similar dynamic is used with sound in *The Conversation.*

8. Emotional Proximity

Emotional proximity can produce a similar dynamic. Loosely equivalent to a novelist's decision to tell a story in the first, second, or third person, emotional proximity reflects how much insight you want viewers to have about the real thoughts and feelings of the characters. This is a very powerful way to create bonding with characters and a powerful area of style. The ramifications of this choice gives your story resonance, yet many writers never even consider this area of stylistic choice.

The Last Emperor is an example of a brilliant use of emotional proximity in the "distant" mode. Not only are there huge sets, great vistas, and many long shots, but even the most personal moments of the main character's life are conveyed impersonally with rigid formality. All of this combines to restate the driving dynamic of the film, which is that the emperor was a person who was never allowed normal emotional intimacy because of his position. Everyone in the film treats him like a pawn of history rather than a human being, and despite the strong sense of compassion viewers develop for the character, they are never allowed to have a real sense of bonding. This emotional dynamic is very potent and gave the film much of its poignancy.

The Age of Innocence also employs a very "distant" emotional proximity which intentionally keeps viewers apart from the world of the story. Using a narrator who is not even in the story adds to this distance, as do the narrator's frequent commentaries on events.

An example of "moderate" emotional proximity is a film like *To Die For,* in which the audience hears Nicole Kidman's thoughts and explanations as the story progresses. The script shifts back and forth from unintentional insights that the characters don't realize she's revealed, to clever omissions and excuses that fool the audience for a while. This allows the audience to have some intimate knowledge of her emotional state while never letting viewers truly identify with her. Again, this mimics the same emotional dynamic which her character provokes in the film, thus intensifying its impact.

"Intimate" emotional proximity is often seen in stories with revealing voice-overs such as *Casino,* or more intimate proximity in scripts like *A Christmas Story,* in which the entire story is not only told, but actually seen through the character's eyes. Set in the thirties, this film is a delightful example of emotional proximity as a young boy agonizes through the ordeals of growing up. The audience actually sees and hears his thoughts and fantasies. "The Wonder Years" employed much of this dynamic on television, although since that narrator was a grown man commenting on his boyhood, it does not have the immediacy of stories experienced solely in the present tense.

Where your script falls on the spectrum of emotional proximity has a lot to do with what kind of hero you're writing about. Idol heroes, and sometimes Lost Souls, often benefit from a degree of emotional distance, while Everyman and Underdog heroes are often enriched by more intimate emotional proximity.

9. Narrative Style

Narrative style has a lot to do with the dynamic created by comparing and contrasting the words and visual images of our story. In some films the two are very much in synch, while in others obvious contrast creates an entirely new dimension in storytelling.

Raising Arizona is a wonderful example of the contrast between words and events. For example, the lead character describes a beautiful sunset while viewers see the tawdriest, shabby domestic scene, yet it is exactly this romantic view of such a shabby world that endears the character to viewers. *All That Jazz* employs the same technique to create a more cynical tone, using the contrast between the choreographer's self-mocking commentary and images of physical exhaustion to convey the depth of his self-destructiveness.

It isn't necessary to have a narrator in order to use this technique. Any characters who look at their experiences from a unique perspective can create wonderful richness through inventive use of style. "Third Rock from the Sun" and *Wings of Desire* use interesting contrasts between what the audience sees, and what the characters feel.

10. Flow

Another arena of style choices has to do with the narrative *flow* of your story. Many scripts employ an invisible connection or juxtaposition between scenes, which means that the script attempts to move through the sequence of scenes without any conspicuous gaps, while a more conscious flow can create strong curiosity or suspense for viewers.

Much of *Pulp Fiction*'s impact came from its unique sequence of events, and Harold Pinter's *Betrayal* tells a fairly simple story in an intriguing way by reversing the chronological order. Both the book and the film of *The World According to Garp* used this stylistic device by making viewers wait a conspicuously long time to find out about the death of Robin Williams' child after a car accident. By contrast, *Charade* maintained both it's mystery and it's fun by employing a constant series of surprises.

You should make a conscious choice about which kind of narrative flow would be most beneficial for your script. By your final drafts, you should know whether (or when) to give or withhold knowledge and whether (or when) to tell the audience the truth. This will enhance your story roller coaster and give emphasis to key moments.

Tone: The Sum of the Parts

The total sum of your style choices will ultimately create a script's *tone*, which is one of the ways writers can convey how *they* feel about the story they're telling.

Consider the difference between *Dangerous Liaisons* and *Valmont*. Both of these films presented the same story. However, their tones differ completely. *Dangerous Liaisons* is a portrait of a sharp, brittle, hard, dangerous, and dramatic world; which can be seen in the characters, their behavior, their motivation, their language, and even their costumes. In contrast, *Valmont* was a much softer, more human presentation of the same tale. The characters, goals, and motives are more accessible, and this was reflected in the softer colors, less starched costumes, and more identifiable characterizations.

How To Determine Your Style

Your dramatic center is the compass that you use to create and combine individual style elements without losing sight of their harmony and function within the whole. If you understand the core dynamics of your idea, your visceral sensation gives you great clarity on the logical and emotional aspects of your plot, character, and momentum devices, telling you what stylistic choices will enhance your script.

But to express that visceral sensation most consistently demands translating it into conscious choices. This allows you to have *unity of presentation* throughout all the layers of your story, which is created by complementary style choices on all levels and layers of the script.

Here are some of the dynamics of your story that can be strengthened with an imaginative use of style, thus making the dramatic equation of your story a visceral experience, not just an intellectualized theme or idea:

1. Intensify the dramatic equation.

2. Convey the hero's values.

3. Enhance the emotional bond with the hero.

4. Emphasize the matchup of hero and obstacle course.

5. Establish the difficulty of the central challenge.

6. Intensify the antagonists' strengths and powers.

7. Separate the hero and "the world."

8. Convey a consistent tone.

9. Create layers of unity throughout all elements of the roller coaster.

10. Express your unique "signature" as a writer.

Q U E S T I O N S

Here are some questions to help you make sure that you are using style to enhance the core of your story:

1. What is the dramatic center of your story? the dramatic equation? What style choices will intensify them?

2. What kind of qualities do the emotions/sensations have?
   Prolonged and slow, like suspense?
   Sudden, shocking, or jagged, like surprise?
   Lilting or pastoral, like happiness?

3. What kind of contrasts of emotional states would best create your desired roller coaster?

4. What would best convey the essence of the hero's world and his world view?

5. What kind of bond between viewers and characters do you want to build?

6. Where on the style spectrum is your story most effective?

7. What are the significant revealing details that convey key information in your story?

8. Consider whether you are using the following:
   Scale: big or small?
   Proportion: norm or flipped?
   Proximity: close or far (physically and emotionally)?
   Authorial distance: first, second, third person?
   Color: Is it consistent with other elements?
   Texture: What adjective describes your script?
   Rhythm: fast, slow, or varied?
   Duration: Would changes in duration enhance your idea?
   Flow: smooth or choppy?

9. Is your style streamlined, transparent, or theatrical?

10. How are you using style to enhance your dramatic equation?

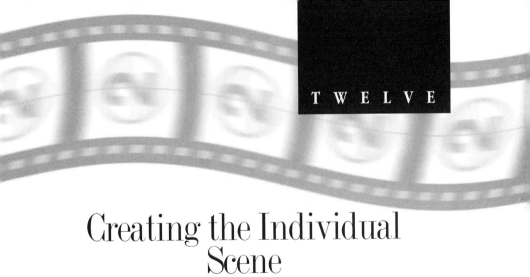

Creating the Individual Scene

Once you understand the major components of story roller coasters, it's time to construct your own. Depending on what form of film or television you write for, that means creating somewhere between 15 and 70 individual scenes. Just as each cell in your body performs its own function while containing your entire DNA code, each scene in your script must hold the audience's moment-to-moment interest while contributing to the overall dynamics of the roller coaster so viewers will experience your dramatic center.

Because you always keep these dual functions in mind, writing a compelling screenplay shares many similarities with an architect creating a home. To be successful, you must deal with both aspects of your discipline: The structural logic needed to create the home and an awareness of what impacts the buyers' subjective reaction.

In order to succeed, an architect must understand the physical realities to build a sound home, but no one decides to buy a home because they think it has great pressured steel beams. Instead they're drawn to the beautiful windows, the size of the rooms, and the detailed woodwork—the experiential details on the surface which cannot exist without a firm foundation underneath.

The same is true for screenwriters. Knowing how to build a story roller coaster is equivalent to the architect's technical knowledge. This analytical view is *author logic*. However, the sensations that determine whether an audience finds the roller-coaster material emotionally satisfying are similar to the buyer's concerns. That subjective reaction is the *audience experience*. Although audience experience ultimately depends on the decisions made through author logic, its concerns are very different. A successful writer must deal with both in every scene of the script.

We have already talked about how to determine what "author logic" elements you need to convey to the audience in your scenes. Now let's talk about screenwriting techniques that can make your "audience experience" a compelling reading experience as well.

Constructing a Scene

As a screenwriter, you have two tools with which to create your story and your script. They are stage directions and dialogue, which together form scenes. Here are some thoughts to keep in mind as you create those individual units of your story:

1. Every Scene Must Have a Clearly Defined Story Pillar

Each scene in your completed script should have a clear purpose, both in terms of advancing the audience's understanding of the story and in contributing to the overall construction of the roller-coaster design. The audience experience function of a scene is to convey the story information necessary to track the logical and emotional progression of change. For example, one scene may convey the fact that a couple has broken up, while the next might convey the husband's sadness. However, scenes also have a structural purpose as well. The author logic or structural function is creating the right-height story pillar for that section of the roller coaster. To further the above example, the scene in which the couple splits up could provide a big spike of surprise, while the following scene of quiet regret provides a momentary lull. That's why it's so helpful to have a sense of the script's structure.

In order to address the audience experience aspect of your scene, you must be very clear about the key changes in your story, the plot and character arcs, the central idea of what the characters' motives and goals are, what is at stake in this scene, who wins and who loses, and what the characters' attitudes are toward the result. To service the author logic, you must make sure that you know how high the story pillar is supposed to be, and how you intend to achieve that height.

2. No Story Pillar Can Be Neutral

Because of the audience's hunger for new information and emotional attachment, a scene's impact can't be neutral. The audience always experiences the next pillar as higher or lower than the previous one. Therefore, you should avoid including scenes that only set up future events, because if the audience can't find a clear story pillar within the scene, they will feel a sense of disappointment, causing their experience of the roller coaster to sag.

The audience wants reassurances that the effort will be worthwhile, that the message conveyed in the dramatic equation is valid, that the author knows the world of the story, and that the effort to become equally familiar will prove worthwhile.

You need to establish authority, credibility, and trustworthiness. An audience can sense a storyteller not in command as a horse can sense a rider's apprehension. They will sense whether they can trust the storyteller, if they are being taken somewhere new and different, and if the story has something worthwhile to say. The moment the author gives inaccurate, useless, or inconsistent information, the audience begins to withdraw, stopping whatever momentum there was.

3. Every Story Pillar Should Contribute To the Dramatic Equation

If you were doing a quick outline of your script and were told to boil each scene down to one sentence, that sentence would probably be the story pillar of the scene, the key piece of information to which you are consciously drawing the audience's attention. Although they may not be aware of it, viewers are looking for that story pillar, that click of the scene as they put together the mosaic of your story, and if they do not discover it, they will lack a sense of completion by the end of the scene.

Another danger emerges as the viewers look for the scene click: If they don't find it, they may assign that significance to some other aspect of the scene and thereby accidentally twist the focus or meaning of your story.

The way to guard against such misunderstandings is to make sure every scene in your script has a clear purpose, both within the audience's experience and the author logic. The "headline" is the obvious, face-value purpose of the scene in terms of audience experience, while the "small print" is the author logic, structural function, which may or may not even be apparent to the viewers. However, even if it is, then it should seem secondary to the headline function, which is the audience's conscious understanding of the story pillar at the time.

4. Every Scene Should Address the Four Audience Needs

Each scene must also fulfill at least one of the four audience needs of *new information, bonding, conflict resolution,* and *completion.* In fact, as a general rule, the more you can address each one in a scene, the more intrigued the audience will be. However, when trying to address more than one need, make sure they work in coordination, rather than competing for the audience's attention. One good way to do that is to decide which one should function as the headline of the scene while the others serve as small print.

5. Come in Late and Leave Early

Screen time is valuable, and the audience's hunger for new information is strong. Therefore you should only include the information the audience will perceive as directly related to your story pillar. Viewers quickly become impatient when a scene is padded. The more you can trim your scene down to just the core information, the richer the story will seem and the stronger the momentum. Audiences quickly realize that they have to stay on their toes with a story that moves briskly, and briskness alone will create a sense of eagerness and curiosity

6. Avoid Clutter

For the same reason, avoid clutter. Filling screen time with trivia undercuts the scene's impact, so unless it is somehow important to your overall roller coaster, keep it to a minimum. For example, a scene in which a group of people are introducing themselves probably does not contain enough new information to be worth screen time unless, for example, one of the characters uses a name the audience knows is fake, or someone is abnormally shy. That kind of information could be valuable for arousing curiosity and/or advancing the storyline, but usually it is tedious and should be cut.

Writers often have trouble streamlining their scenes, and their reasoning is "that's what would happen in real life." But forget real life—the screen is not real life. Instead, it is a distillation of life, and you should present distilled information. Occurrences in real life can last any amount of time, but your screenplay can only last approximately 120 minutes. You must evaluate every word in your scenes with that limitation in mind.

The audience is looking for direction and will often take things literally, so avoid filling your opening scenes with decorative clutter and instead provide information that deals directly with the story.

7. *Keep Exposition To a Minimum*

In many ways, exposition is like that initial time spent on a roller coaster when the cars are pulled uphill until they are high enough to let the fun part of the ride begin. It's not the most fun part of the ride, but it's necessary.

In a story roller coaster, you want to keep the exposition to an absolute minimum, especially at the outset when the audience already feels an innate sense of resistance, as we've already discussed.

8. *The Transitions Between Scenes Are Important*

You should give careful thought to how your scenes progress in transition from one to the next. It may involve the last line of dialogue in one scene and the first line in the next, or an action scene flowing into an exposition scene, or one action scene bumping into another one.

Juxtapose your scenes in a logically evocative way. Notice how they "feel" next to each other. Each scene needs to lead to the next, tracking some aspect of change within the story. The connection can be a straightforward cause and effect or something more subtle than that. But scenes that come later in the script must answer the questions in the audience's mind. The scene flow should also illuminate your story arc, connecting scenes in a way that makes the changes in the story seem natural or at least credible. The sequence of plot events conveys the rational logic of your story, while the pattern of emotional change that a lead character undergoes is the emotional arc of your story.

You can also create sequences linked by rhythm and pacing, as in the garage dance sequence in *Footloose;* by location, as in *Two for the Road;* by time, in period and contemporary sequences, as in *The French Lieutenant's Woman;* or by intent, as in the training sequences in *Rocky.*

Stage Directions

Stage directions are the first major tool used to convey information to readers. They are responsible for conveying the visual information in your scene.

Audience members who may someday see your work on the screen may never know the power (or weakness) of your stage directions, but since it can have immense impact on readers who may choose your script to film, you need to make sure that you employ writing techniques that will maximize your big picture creative decisions. There are some key things you need to remember about stage directions:

1. Keep Stage Directions Concise

By saying you should *keep your stage directions short,* I don't mean that you shouldn't have a very clear sense of what the scenes look like, how the characters behave, and what kind of setting there is. You must see every scene vividly in your mind; the writer who can't see or hear the scene taking place is going to have difficulty making it come alive for readers. However, there is a big difference between seeing each detail in your mind and forcing the reader to envision the scene exactly as you would like to see it filmed.

Remember that the stage directions for a script are only the "instruction manual" to make a movie. Their only function is to create the kinds of sensations and feelings in readers that make them feel as though they are seeing the completed movie in their minds. Their function is *not* to describe every thought that goes through your mind while imagining a scene; that's not necessary to understanding your story, nor is it the best way to share it.

This writing flaw is most often caused by writers' attempts to describe the scene precisely as envisioned in their minds. It's as though they believe the only way to capture the power of the moment is to describe every element of the scene in minute detail. Ironically, weighing your script down with unnecessary detail will work against your desire to make the reader feel the vitality of the moment.

There are many reasons why you should learn to restrain yourself. One is that conveying the precise images in your head into someone else's head is impossible. You can convey the tone, the mood, and a general sense of location, for instance, but *exactly* what the table looks like is too detailed and still guarantees nothing about the reader's reaction to your tale. Think about your own experience: a friend describes someone to you, complete with gestures and vocal expressions; you think you have an accurate mental picture, but then you meet the person and realize that your image was completely wrong.

Another reason for restraining yourself is more practical than creative. Most people in this business have so much reading to do in their work that thick, long paragraphs in a script cause their enthusiasm to drop dramatically. They assume as a result of long, painful experience that thick prose means the writer has been unable to organize the information according to its importance, and that they are about to plunge into long passages where only a few pieces of information are vital. The emotional power of the scene can be lost as the result of overwritten stage directions, and in the process, author credibility suffers. The reader begins to wonder, "If the writer doesn't know what's really important, how likely is it that this story will ultimately pay off ?"

2. Focus on Conveying the Essence of the Scene

Rather than describing every image that comes to mind when you think of a scene, try selecting one or two *revealing details* that convey the rest. For example, if you are writing a scene about a woman who is pretending to be rich, you don't need to describe every item of clothing she's wearing. You'll be more effective by simply mentioning that the sleeves of her silk blouse are frayed or that the price tag from the thrift shop can be seen on her collar.

Leave room for the reader's imagination to intermingle with your revealing details; the interaction encourages readers to personalize their involvement. Just as radio was the "theater of the mind," allowing the audience to grab hold of a scene and fill in images that were most relevant to their experience, short pertinent stage directions let your readers imagine their own most vivid image of "a greasy spoon" or "a millionaire's mansion."

3. Use Visually Evocative Words

Another way to convey the essence of a scene quickly is through imaginative *word* choice. There's a huge difference in the visual images created by the phrases "A boat passes by" and "A white yacht glides past."

Similarly, where you choose to set your scene, as well as how you describe that setting, can add texture and tension. For example, a love scene in a library will feel very different from the same dialogue spoken on the beach.

4. Use Emotionally Evocative Words

Using verbs that convey attitude and atmosphere can also add impact to your script. However, try to focus your efforts on strong descriptions of visual information, rather than on adding lots of "running commentary." The latter can often seem too smart-alecky and distracting. There's another problem, too; if the characters and dialogue aren't as interesting as the commentary (which happens fairly often), the characters will seem even blander by contrast.

5. Create a Sense of Movement and Action

It is important that the essential energy of your story be conveyed in the visual images of your screenplay rather than in the dialogue. It's important to convey the major actions and reactions that the characters have, but long, detailed descriptions will actually work against the sense of speed and excitement needed to make those scenes work best.

As a result, some writers limit themselves to two-line descriptions in each paragraph, even if there must be ten such paragraphs to describe the scene. This concise style is particularly important for action scenes, which need to seem fast and exciting.

6. Write Stage Directions in the Present Tense

Since you want to bring readers into your world, you don't want to distance them with past tense. Writing stage directions in the present tense creates greater immediacy and impact, while the past tense constantly separates readers from the moment and keeps them at arm's length from the story.

7. Don't Include Camera Angles

Choosing the camera angle is the director's job. If you insist on making those choices, you don't allow the director's imagination to grab hold of the script and see it through his or her own eyes. Additionally, the images that are so exciting for you because of the information in your negative space may actually work against the director's sense of excitement or may be less compelling than those which could be imagined if your stage directions weren't hampering his or her ability to come to the script without preconceptions.

The only time to include a camera angle is when it is essential to understanding a scene. Making it clear to readers that the audience will see a man's legs during the murder sequence but never his face may be enough reason, but even then it's better to describe what the scene would look like rather than what camera angle should be used to achieve that look.

Dialogue

The second major tool you have with which to convey information in your screenplay is *dialogue,* the language that the audience will hear on the screen.

On the stage, the fact that there are physical constraints of time and place demand that dialogue carry a great deal of the dramatic "weight." But the screen is predominantly a visual medium, so words rarely have the same impact as they do on the stage. As a result, conventional wisdom claims that dialogue is not of primary importance in a screenplay; in fact, Hitchcock has been credited with saying, "Build your screenplay first, then add dialogue." That may be a bit extreme, but the point is that the real power of a screenplay comes from the dramatic equation and the overall roller-coaster ride, not the conversation.

However, because it creates a "first impression" of your screenplay, dialogue is of great importance. The way a writer uses dialogue is very revealing. Good dialogue shows that a writer understands people and has an ear for how they talk. Bad dialogue instantly impairs author credibility. The moment professionals read a script with stilted, talky, or overly theatrical dialogue, they begin to suspect the writer does not have the skill to create a compelling script. As soon as those doubts set in, the writer is working uphill to prove him- or herself.

Here are some tips for writing credible dialogue:

1. Characters Should Have Distinctive Voices

Most writers have a "voice" that permeates their entire script (including stage directions) unless they make a conscious and determined effort to differentiate. As a result, all their characters tend to talk with the same rhythm, pacing, humor, sensibility, and vocabulary.

Creating a distinctive *voice* for each character is important and can be a powerful way to make characters come alive. Think about Al Pacino's character in *Scent of a Woman,* Archie Bunker in "All in the Family," Katharine Hepburn and Humphrey Bogart in *African Queen,* or each character in *Guarding Tess.* A lot of the fun in sitcoms comes from distinctive (and unchanging) characters, often most vividly expressed in their dialogue. Some examples are "Seinfeld," "Murphy Brown," "The Nanny," and "Fraser."

A character's voice is conveyed through word choice, phrasing, mannerisms, attitudes, and tone. One way to practice writing distinctive dialogue is to imagine a specific person conveying the information you want your character to say. For example, how would your best friend give street directions? How would your favorite teacher? Notice different word choices, points of reference, mannerisms, slang. Focus on personal speech styles and try to include and convey those distinctions in your dialogue. Also try comparing each of your characters to the other. How would your hero say a line? How would the antagonist convey the same information? How would your mother?

2. Know What Your Characters Want to Say

If you are struggling with dialogue in your screenplay, it may be because you aren't really sure what your characters want or need to say. Once you are clear on the characters' intentions and desires, you may find that the words come easily. If not, try asking yourself, "What's the point of this line?" Putting the character's thoughts into your own words, and then translating that idea into the character's unique manner of expression may help give you clarity.

3. Keep Character Voices Consistent

Often characters' voices are clear and distinct at the beginning of the screenplay, when the writer's concentration is on establishing the characters. However, as soon as the plot begins, the characters lose their distinctiveness and become stick figures, expressing themselves in a very generic way. So make a special effort to create and maintain your characters' voices throughout, because that will significantly strengthen the script's credibility.

4. Dialogue Should be Consistent With the Story's Style

Similar to the choices available to you in the overall style of your script, you can choose to make your dialogue "transparent," "theatrical," or "streamlined."

Transparent dialogue sounds like everyday speech and is usually the best choice unless there is a conspicuously important aspect you want to emphasize. Transparent dialogue keeps the focus on the information being conveyed rather than on the "packaging," as anything other than realistic dialogue tends to call attention to itself. Keep the dialogue on screen focused on new information. Cluttering the movie with social chatter, unless you have an important point to make, is not a good use of screen time.

Theatrical dialogue calls attention to itself, whether it's the wild chatter of Peter O'Toole in *The Stuntman*, nearly all the characters in *A Clockwork Orange*, the bold absurdism of *Airplane, Ruthless People*, "Beavis and Butthead," or "Green Acres," or any other stylized use of words. The further away something is from the norm, the more attention it draws, so you want to use such a theatrical element with precision and clarity.

Streamlined dialogue is minimal, unnaturally terse, even staccato. Examples of streamlined dialogue might be *Casablanca; Double Indemnity;* many movies in the film noire style; *The Good, the Bad, and the Ugly;* and Arnold Schwarzenegger's consciously abrupt dialogue in *Terminator 2: Judgement Day*. Many action characters tend to speak in such a manner. The style of speech emphasizes and intentionally reinforces the difference between the character and ordinary people.

No matter what style of dialogue you use, it should always enhance and enrich your dramatic center and the overall tone of your story.

5. Dialogue Should Convey Attitude

Dialogue that adequately conveys information but no attitude seems lifeless and artificial. That's because in real life people have attitudes about everything. Even a quick question like "What time is it?" can convey attitude—such as "I must be really late" or "Isn't this lecture over yet?"

Dialogue can also convey characters' attitudes toward themselves. Characters express themselves very differently depending on how comfortable they are saying what's being said. For example, the words and phrasing a shy woman would use to invite someone to dinner are quite different from the same invitation extended by a bold, confident woman.

6. Action Speaks Louder Than Words

If you've ever tried to express yourself during an argument or when your heart is filled with despair, you know how difficult it is even to put your feelings into words, let alone well-chosen ones. To expect characters to do that makes them seem contrived.

The reason for this type of impact is that, in general, dialogue is better at expressing thoughts than emotions. If you intend to convey an emotion, consider whether there's an action or gesture that would express the feeling more effectively than language. Also think about whether something should be included in stage directions rather than in dialogue, or if it really needs to be conveyed to the audience at all.

Some writers are convinced that readers cannot understand the character or story unless they are told every thought, but, as with stage directions, usually that much detail detracts from rather than enriches a script.

7. Avoid Long Speeches

Although a few big speeches can work on stage, long speeches on screen tend to make viewers' feel restless. Because film is a visual medium, audiences take in information far more easily with their eyes than with their ears, so even well-done long speeches, such as the one at the end of *Presumed Innocent,* are risky at best, and very hard to make convincing on the page.

Dialogue must have a realistic flow. There's nothing more awkward than a character asking a question followed by a long declarative sentence, and then having the other character respond to the question. That's not how people really talk so it seems stilted and artificial.

Another dialogue technique to avoid is two-fers. These are what I call lines of dialogue that combine two dissimilar thoughts into one speech. "Go to hell, Jake. (pause) By the way, did you stop at the store?" is an example of a two-fer. This manner of speaking should be avoided unless you are using it deliberately to establish a character's distracted or confused state of mind. Two-fers convey the impression that the author doesn't know how to write dialogue, causing an immediate decline in author credibility.

To avoid constructing two-fers, separate them, if only with a quick one-word response from the other character.

8. Listen to Your Dialogue Out Loud

If you have any opportunity to hear actors, or even just friends, read your script out loud, take it. You will quickly learn much more about what works and what doesn't work than anything you can imagine in your head. If that seems too horrifying to contemplate, at least read it out loud to yourself. Often you can feel right away that a speech is too lengthy, or artificial, or contrived as soon as you hear someone say the words.

Q U E S T I O N S

Here are some questions to help ensure that you are creating vivid individual scenes:

1. SCENES

1. What is the story pillar of your scene?
   Is it a load-bearing one?
   What is the headline, author logic function?
   What is the small print, audience experience function?
   What is the scene click?

2. Where is this pillar in the overall design of your roller coaster? Up?
   Down? Why?
   What speed?
   Is it a key moment?
   Does it change the direction, speed, etc.?
   How?

3. What is at stake in this scene?

4. What is each character's goal in the scene?
   What is the attitude?
   Does it advance the heroes' internal motivation? External plans?
   Who wants what?
   Who gets what they want and why?
   Who doesn't, and why?
   What is their reaction to the win or loss?

5. How does your scene address the need for . . .
   New information?
   Bonding?
   Conflict resolution?
   Completion?

6. How does it advance your plot?
   Characterizations?
   Momentum?

7. How is momentum established or created?

8. Is anything set up?
   Is anything paid off ?
   As foreshadowing?
   As a planted seed? If it's a planted seed, how is it disguised?

9. What questions does the scene answer?
   What new questions does it plant in viewers' minds?
   What are the central "How" or "Why" questions?
   Is it a "How" or "Why" story?

10. Does the setting heighten the emotional impact?
    Style?
    Dialogue?
    Stage directions?

11. How does this scene connect to your dramatic equation and your dramatic center?

2. STAGE DIRECTIONS

12. Are they as short as you can possibly make them?

13. What is the essence of each scene?
What are the revealing details?

14. What are you doing to make them visually powerful?
Emotionally intense?

15. How is information visually conveyed?

3. DIALOGUE

16. What are your characters trying to say?
What are they comfortable saying?

17. Are your character voices distinctive?

18. What is being conspicuously unsaid?
Does it need to be said?
Would it be more powerful as an action?
Is it more powerful in silence?

19. What dialogue style is best for your script?
Transparent?
Streamlined?
Theatrical?

20. Have you heard your dialogue out loud?
What discoveries did you make that you didn't see while writing
the dialogue at the keyboard?

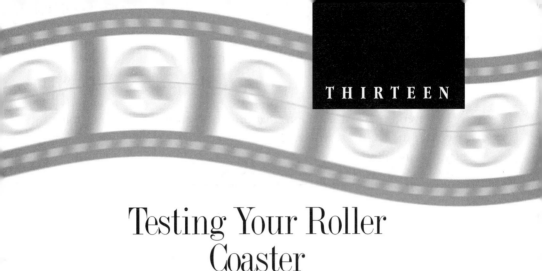

Testing Your Roller Coaster

Now you've built your roller coaster, element by element. But before you open it to the public at large, you need to do some test runs to make sure that it creates the sensations it was designed to deliver.

There are two things you want to check. One is whether the highs and lows, curves and twists, textures and speeds all function as you intended; the other is to make sure that the roller-coaster ride, even if it functions as designed, provides an enveloping experience for your riders.

The intended design of your roller coaster, as well as the resulting choices you made to construct it, are a reflection of your *author logic*. For example, your roller coaster may have been intended to have this kind of design:

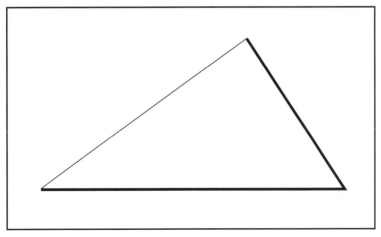

Figure 13-1   Author Logic

However, the actual sensations that people have when riding your roller coaster are the *audience experience,* and the roller coaster they actually experience may look like this:

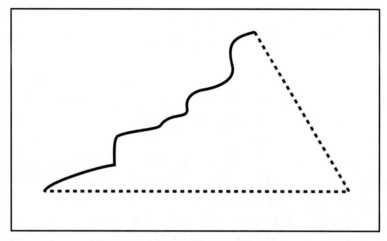

Figure 13-2   Audience Experience

Ideally the tracks of those two roller coasters should be the same, but often that is not the case, especially in first drafts. In fact, it is normal to have at least small discrepancies, and sometimes there are major differences. Those gaps between the roller coaster you intended and the ride the audience actually takes are the "Bermuda Triangle" of stories.

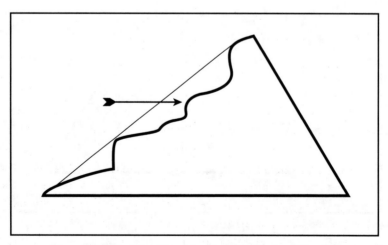

Figure 13-3   The "Bermuda Triangle" of Stories

Your goal is to create a screenplay where author logic and audience experience are the same. Therefore, after you complete a draft of your screenplay, you must evaluate whether there is a difference between author logic and audience experience, and if so, where and why. Then you can proceed to make whatever changes are necessary.

The main reason there can be such "black holes" is not because it's impossible to synch up these two lines, but because most writers don't even recognize that the difference between author logic and audience experience may exist. You must always be aware that the essence of the story experience takes place in the viewers' heads, not on the page or on the screen. No matter how eloquent a case you make for why an audience *should* feel a certain way, "the customer is always right." It is your responsibility to make sure that you have consciously addressed this challenge and used your craftsmanship to ensure the ride that you, the artist, intended to create.

When a Roller Coaster Doesn't Work

The reason Bermuda Triangle gaps exist between the writer's intention and the audience experience is that the writer guessed incorrectly about the height of the story pillars. The writer has overestimated the intensity of the audience's reaction to a piece of story information, and viewers sense that they are supposed to be having a more powerful reaction than they are actually having.

When that happens, the audience feels an unsettling kind of sinking sensation, almost like hitting an "air pocket," which disrupts their concentration, momentarily distancing them from the story and hampering the overall emotional build.

Think about your own experiences as an audience member. You know the sensation. You're sitting there, enjoying a movie, and suddenly a moment feels false or contrived. You feel a small internal jolt, almost as though you're losing your balance for a second. You also feel let down, disappointed, and a little wary about whether the ride is going to falter again. It's a distinctly unpleasant feeling for viewers, and one that writers want to avoid at all costs.

Yet if the sensation is so obvious, why do most writers make this mistake? Because it's never possible to take a first-time ride on a roller coaster you've built, and it's that first roller-coaster ride, the "virgin reaction," that evokes the clearest sensations.

Virgin Reaction

When someone initially reads a script or sees a movie, they have a virgin reaction because they have no knowledge—and therefore no expectations—of upcoming story events. During that first ride, the viewers' logic and emotions experience the story exactly as it is, with their gut reactions indicating clearly what is not working.

Among the sensations the audience may feel during a virgin reaction are the click of recognition when they realize the importance of a load-bearing pillar, the "tightening of the screw" sensation when a story pillar adds to the mounting dramatic tension, or the "ugh!" when a story pillar conspicuously fails to reach its potential height.

If you have read someone else's script, you know how easy it is to see what's working and what's not. However, read that script a second time and you will see how different your reactions are. Some things that were confusing the first time won't bother you the second and vice versa. That's because you have a sense of where the story is going, and your mind begins to fill in the blanks.

Virgin reactions are extremely valuable because they enable the writer to be most in touch with what an audience feels. Yet losing touch with the virgin reaction is an unavoidable part of the creative process, because writers who know their own script well enough to anticipate events can never experience their own story from the audience's point of view. It's what is meant by a writer being "too close" to the work.

So there's the essence of your dilemma: If you can never get on and take the ride for yourself, how can you tell if your roller coaster provides the ride you intended? How do you overcome the built-in subjectivity you have as the writer? The answer is you have to get accurate feedback from someone riding your roller coaster for the first time.

Letting Others Take a "Test Ride"

In order to make the most of the secondhand information you will get when you ask someone to read your script, you need to have a clear idea of what you want your audience/readers to feel as they go through your story. Then you must assess how well your intended roller-coaster design matches what your readers experience.

Here are some guidelines for making sure that you get the most accurate feedback possible:

1. Know What You Want Your Audience to Feel

The entire basis for your roller-coaster design is knowing precisely how you want your audience to feel, not just by the end of your screenplay, but at every stage along the way. What emotions do you want your audience to experience, in what order, and to what intensity? Be prepared to articulate these answers.

If you've done your homework, you should have a very clear notion of what you want the audience to be thinking and feeling at any given moment in your story, what questions you want them to have, what assumptions you want them to make, whose side you want them to take in arguments, and what expectations you want them to form by what point in the story. As though you could graph your story, you should know exactly where the highs and lows should be and what causes them. That is the pattern that creates the story roller coaster for the audience, so you should know exactly what responses would create the ideal ride. If, as you listen to the feedback, you hear answers that are different from the ones you expected, you will be able to locate the exact placement of your Bermuda Triangle.

2. Choose Your Audience Carefully

In order to trust the feedback you get, you must really trust the person you ask to read your script, in terms of overall aesthetic taste, ability to articulate reactions, and credibility.

Pick someone who you think will tell you his or her true reactions, not just what you want to hear. It's also a good idea to pick someone who likes the same kind of movies you do. By doing this, you are not trying to "stack the deck" by asking people whose responses are usually in keeping with yours, but someone whose sensibilities you trust.

3. Know What Audience You are Writing For

Know who and what your intended audience is, and be honest with yourself: Is the reader you've selected a good sampling of that audience? If your story is geared toward young teens, is your grandmother really the best person to go on the test ride? If you decide to show it to her anyway, should you panic if she thinks it's too "silly"?

4. Word Your Questions Neutrally

It's tempting to ask your readers, "Did you like my script?", but most of the time this doesn't yield useful information. One reason is that most people won't want to hurt your feelings, and such loaded language makes it hard for them to be completely honest about any weaknesses. Even if they do like it, such vague questions really only ask the reader, "How does it compare to your idea of what the story should be?"

So be specific, but try not to use judgmental words. Ask questions that people aren't hesitant to answer. For example, don't ask, "Were you bored?" Rather ask, "What did you expect to happen on page 100?" That kind of neutral question allows them to respond with specific observations rather than judgments and will make the feedback much more valuable.

What you need to know as clearly as possible is what the roller-coaster ride felt like to them—where they went up, where they went down, where it felt slow or fast, where they found the sensations satisfying and where they did not. You need to know what they were feeling and when in order to track whether your roller coaster is creating the structure that you want the riders to perceive.

5. Translate the Answers

George Bernard Shaw once wrote, "Most people can tell you there's a problem, but it takes a genius to tell you how to fix it." People can usually tell when there's something wrong with a script, and they can even spot the moment where the problem becomes obvious. But trying to determine exactly what's causing the problem and what needs to be changed can be a lot more difficult.

So ask for and listen to your readers' reactions, but don't take their comments or suggestions too literally. Instead, like a doctor examining a patient, focus your energy on hearing the symptoms described rather than accepting their self-diagnosis at face value.

Even professionals can find it difficult to express their instinctive reactions to screenplays, so you can imagine how hard it may be for a layman to express thoughts accurately. Consequently, you have to act as a translator.

For example, if a reader says, "I don't think this character is working very well" or "I don't believe the character would do that," don't let your pride get you too focused on semantics. Rather, hear the important information; something about that characterization isn't working for this reader.

Focus on understanding the essence of readers' comments. You can then attempt to get more specific by using your dramatic equation to pin down the problem.

The way this technique works is that you suggest a scenario in which all your story elements remain the same except the one in question. Ask the reader how changing that one in a certain way would affect his or her reaction. For example, you could say, "If I kept the plot events the same but made the character more likable, would that fix the problem?" or "What if I kept the same characterization but changed the plot?" The resulting discussions can help you pinpoint the real issue.

6. Listen Selectively

Notes that help you build the roller coaster you intend to create are very useful. So are notes that confirm problem areas that have been bugging you. It's especially important to pay attention if you get the same note saying the same thing from more than one person. Even if the feedback contradicts your author logic, you need to remember that audience experience, as with beauty, is in the "eye of the beholder."

7. Listen Critically

However, it's also important to remember that you can "never please all of the people all of the time." If the notes you get are telling you to build a different roller coaster from the one you intended, you should ponder extensively before you change your overall roller-coaster design.

The reason people may be giving you notes that would result in a different roller coaster is that they may be responding to their own dramatic center within the topic. As we've discussed before, people can have very different and unique dramatic centers because of the experiences and world view contained in their own negative spaces; therefore, suggestions to change your roller-coaster design may be prompted by their dramatic center rather than a failure of your roller coaster. If their dramatic center is not the same as yours, their notes will always lead you to build their version of the roller coaster rather than your own.

8. Recognize the Difference Between Objective Observation and Subjective Preferences

All people have their own taste in entertainment, which is why some people dislike a movie even if it's a box office smash. They simply don't enjoy that kind of topic, or roller-coaster ride, and no matter how well built that roller coaster is, their basic reaction is the same. So it's important that you understand whether the comments you are receiving are the result of established preferences or specific observations on your individual script.

For example, if you have friends who don't enjoy children's literature and don't think they are particularly good at responding to it, don't give that type of script to them. They probably wouldn't love it no matter how well it was written. On the other hand, even if they're not crazy about that kind of material, their specific observations about where it held their attention or whether they found the characters empathetic could still be useful.

Many writers assume that anyone will like a good script, or, conversely, that it is possible to write a script that everyone in the world will like. However, that simply is not true. It's vital to remember that you can't please everyone. No matter how compelling a roller coaster is, some people will not enjoy the ride, because of preexisting tastes and preferences that have nothing to do with your specific script. The result is that you could write exactly the script you wanted and they might not like it, or you could have failed to build the roller coaster you intended but they liked the ride they took.

9. Ask Why

That's why you must ask for specifics from your reader. Don't settle for "yes" or "no" answers or first impressions because those are only the tips of the iceberg in terms of how they really responded to your material. It also makes it too easy for you to misunderstand the real meaning of their feedback.

Make sure you ask "Why?"—as in "Why were you surprised?" or "Why did you think the couple would break up?" The answers can be enormously useful. Rather than simply getting a reaction, you get to the root of the reaction, which gives you much greater clarity about how they experienced your screenplay.

For example, if your discussion stays on the "Did you like it—yes or no?" level, you may interpret a response like "I didn't believe the character would do that" as a major disagreement with your story, thus assuming a huge Bermuda Triangle. However, if you can get your readers to be more specific and articulate, you might discover the only reason they didn't believe it was the way the dialogue was written, or because of an assumption they developed about the character which you had not intended. That kind of revelation helps you realize that the gap isn't nearly as great as you first feared.

The discussion may reveal a different kind of insight as well. Your readers may say they didn't like a scene, which might sound as though the roller coaster didn't deliver the ride you intended at that moment, when the truth is that they may have experienced exactly what you wanted them to feel—-they just didn't happen to like that sensation. Needless to say, that's a crucial distinction, so always do your best to get as much detail about your readers' reactions as possible.

10. Ask Where

It's more important to know where your readers felt various sensations and emotional reactions than to know what their final, cumulative opinion is. Therefore, you can either literally stop your readers at intervals and ask questions like, "On page 10, what did you think was going to happen?" "How do you feel on page 20?" Or you can ask them those kinds of questions after they've read your whole script.

The first option tends to give you a more accurate picture of their reactions, but one way or the other, you must make sure that you understand exactly where they felt their various reactions.

11. Keep Looking For Your Ideal Reader

My friend Oliver Hailey thought it was crucial to find that one person, that one springboard, whose reaction you could really trust, and then, as he would say, "Listen, listen, listen."

Finding that ideal reader, that person whom you trust as a sounding board, sometimes takes years, but it can make all the difference in the world if you are lucky enough to find the person.

I know from experience. At first I had a hard time writing this book, because I had taught the material so many times. It was difficult for me to be sure I was expressing the ideas on paper clearly to someone who wasn't already familiar with them. Then my very good friend Jan Wildman offered to be my sounding board, and my entire sense of writing the book changed overnight!

Suddenly I didn't have to spend emotional or intellectual energy wondering if a segment was working, or which order ideas should be in. I knew Jan's taste and understanding of the material was completely fresh yet accurate, so I suddenly had a mirror whose reflection I could trust. I also had faith in her honesty and kindness. I knew that she would tell me the truth, but I also knew that she would not laugh at me (something that all writers fear!). The point is, I felt safe creatively and emotionally, and the book really took off after that.

QUESTIONS TO ASK YOURSELF

Here are sample questions that you might mull over in relation to your script. The questions you need to ask will be specific to your screenplay, but these may get you started:

1. What roller coaster did you intend to build?

2. What emotional reactions do you want readers to have?

3. Where are your intended highs and lows?
   Built on what expectations, preferences, doubts?

4. What do you want them to feel at the beginning of the story?
   In the middle?
   At each key event?
   At the pivotal moment?
   At the climax?
   At the end result?

5. Where should the audience feel surprise?
   Curiosity?
   Suspense?

6. Where should the audience feel hope?
   Dread?
   Excitement?

7. What questions should they be asking?
   Where should they find the answers?

8. When should they feel drawn to the characters, and when repelled?

9. How should they feel at the end?
   What should they want to happen?

10. What should they think is the point of the story?
    Should they agree with your dramatic equation or not?

QUESTIONS TO ASK YOUR READERS

Here are some sample questions for your reader(s). You should already know exactly what you want to hear in response.

1. What is this story about?
   Tell me the story in your own words.

2. What first got your interest? Why?
   When did you lose interest? Why?
   On page 10, what did you expect to happen?
   On page 20? 30? 40? (or whatever pages apply)
   Did you want it to happen?
   Why or why not?

3. Did this script focus on the aspect of the story you found most interesting?
   If not, where would you have liked to see it go?
   Where did you expect it to go?
   Would you have enjoyed that more?
   Why?

4. What new information did you learn from "X" scene?
   Did it tell you anything new about the world?

5. What do you feel about the characters?
   What emotions did you feel for the hero? Villain?
   Empathy? Sympathy? Disinterest? Why?
   Whose side were you on? Why?
   When did you feel connected to the characters?
   Distanced?

6. What questions were you eager to have answered on page "X"? Why?

7. Did you change your mind about any of the characters as the story progressed?

8. What are the key revelations in the story?
   Were you surprised by anything?
   Confused by anything?

9. What would you say was the message of the story?
   Do you agree with that message?

10. Do you think it was worth telling?
   Why?

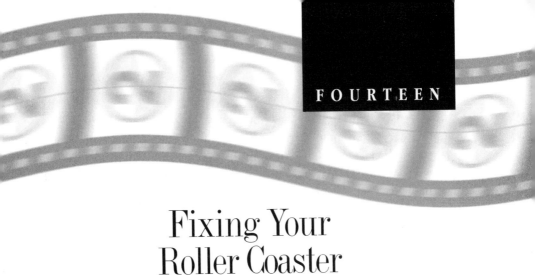

Fixing Your Roller Coaster

Now you have a sense of where your roller coaster is working and where it's not. Chances are that some aspect of your story is not having the impact you intended, and so the final step in creating a great screenplay is the rewrite(s). Here are some techniques for making the most of this final phase of bringing your script to life.

■ Let Your Script Cool ■

Often at this point you have so many conflicting images and impulses, you're not sure which ones to listen to. Which ones are important? Which are most consistent with what you're trying to say?

The best thing you can do when getting ready to rewrite your script is to let it get "cold," which means leaving your script alone for a while so that you can forget as much of your author logic as possible. The goal is to have as much of a virgin, or at least a quasi-virgin, reaction as possible to the material. As a result, the longer you let your script cool, the better. In fact, the ideal is to leave it alone long enough to totally forget what the next line of dialogue is or what the next scene will be, so that you come to the story with as fresh an eye as possible.

However, sometimes it takes months, if not years, for a script to get that cold, and often you simply won't have the time. The next best thing to do is consciously fill your mind with new stimuli to take your mind off the script. Take a vacation. Go to other kinds of movies (not the kind you are working on!). Read books, magazines. Start a project. Take up a hobby. Do anything that is *not* related to your story.

When it's finally time to read your script, that first rereading is a very important step in the process of doing a good rewrite, so do everything you can to get the maximum benefit from the experience. Go someplace where you won't be interrupted, make sure you have as much time as you will need, and then give your full attention to your script, because if you don't it will be weeks, if not months, before you can have such a fresh and enlightening reading of your script again.

Develop a Game Plan

One of the most important things about doing a good rewrite is to keep your big picture goals in mind. Before you start to read your script again, do you have clarity on the sensation that accompanied your dramatic center? Have you had any change of heart about what the core of the story is, or the dramatic equation? Were there any big picture issues that were bugging you when you finished the last draft? Often it is these bigger, deeper issues which change as writers work on a cinematic story, and looking only for small problems will not give you insight into these. It's also very important to give yourself enough time to go through your own creative "question and answer" process so that you are able to understand the significance of the problems that snag your attention, and are genuinely happy and comfortable with the choices you decide to make.

■ Focus on the Big Picture ■

The trick to making the most of this reading is getting a visceral awareness of the whole. It's much more important that you get a sense of the story's overall emotional build than to stop and make corrections. So rather than taking detailed notes or trying to do corrections as you go, just scribble quick "shorthand" signals to remind you of what snagged your attention.

You may think you'll remember what your first reactions were when you go back to fix segments, but you probably won't, especially if you're reading an entire script. However, if you write lengthy notes to yourself, you will lose your ability to really stay on the roller coaster, so just scribble quick notes in the margins, then keep moving forward.

■ Collate Your Notes ■

Once you have indicated your virgin reactions in the margin, you can go through the script more slowly. The point of the second reading is not just to look at the individual problems, but to look for recurring patterns or issues in order to understand the real cause of those problems, not just the symptoms.

Listen to your own instincts, as well as to the notes you've received from others, and try to find the connection between them. Usually a roller coaster fails because of problems with one of the four main audience needs: new information, bonding, conflict resolution, and completion. Which category would most of your notes and concerns fall into? How can you more successfully fulfill those needs and thus draw readers into your story more effectively?

■ Go Back to Your Dramatic Center ■

If you know that something's wrong with your roller coaster, but you're not sure what the cause is, the best thing to do is to go back to the core, to the dramatic center of your story. Have you explored the aspect of this story that most excited you? Have you communicated that aspect of the story to your readers, or do you have to sit there explaining to them what they need to know to make the material on the page compelling? If that's what you're doing, the problem may be that the essence of the story is still in your mind rather than on the page.

If you are too far from your dramatic center, you may mistakenly resort to *short-term solves*. These are solutions that may fix an individual problem but do not contribute to the effectiveness of the overall ride. Not only can short-term solves break up the pattern of tension and release needed for the dramatic structure to work well, but they can also set up expectations the script never delivers on, because the writer never intended to make that promise.

Another problem may be that you never really found your dramatic center, and as a result, your story is lacking that central axis. Your dramatic center determines several crucial aspects of your script, so without it you are probably communicating very mixed messages to your viewers at best.

If you have any doubts about whether you have found your story's dramatic center, here's one way to test to make sure you are on the right track. Take your dramatic center, which is the same quality that separates your hero from the world, and expand each of those opposing value systems to the extreme. Is that the story you want to write about? Does it line up with the separation of the hero and his world? If you play out that difference, is that the world you want to write about? If not, what do you need to change in your story to get it into alignment?

▪ Expand Out to Your Dramatic Equation ▪

Just as you use your dramatic center to create and clarify the essence of your story roller-coaster design, you can also use your dramatic equation to examine whether your execution is bringing your story to life.

One good way is to verbalize the statement of your dramatic equation, then check to make sure that each crucial step in that central arc of change is dramatized in your story. Remember, the dramatic equation is the skeletal statement of your story's essence: "This person, plus this series of events, equals this outcome." Are all of the necessary components there? Does the plot track? Does the character arc track? Are there any missing moments? Is the momentum building toward climax? Is there a pivotal moment when the balance of the equation tilts and change becomes inevitable? Is there a full, cathartic release?

You can also use the dramatic equation to test possible solutions before implementing them. For example, ask yourself such questions as "If I kept the same characterization but changed the character's plan, would that make the script better?" or "If I kept the plotline but changed the character's attitudes and comments, would that be closer to the sensation I'm trying to create?"

▪ Decide Where the Problem Is ▪

No matter what kind of problems you're having in your script, they will always cause a reader to experience the "air-pocket" sensation we discussed in the last chapter. As a result, you can locate where the problem becomes obvious by noticing where in your script the bulk of the notes are located.

There tend to be four major patterns of structural problems:

1. Slow Starts

This kind of roller coaster has a long, slow start before it finally begins to build effectively.

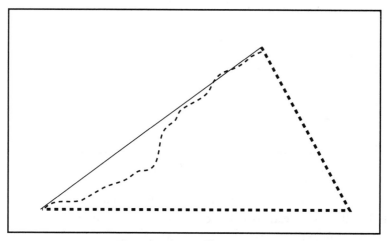

Figure 14-1 "Slow Start"

I experienced this kind of roller-coaster ride when I saw *Jumanji* and *Dead Again*. Even though I eventually became quite involved in the stories, it took a while for my emotional build to start.

This kind of structural flaw is often due to a problem in bonding with the plot or the characters. It can also be caused by a lack of clear direction. Something in the way the story is being told isn't compelling enough to help the audience get past their resistance and on board the roller coaster, so listen carefully to your instincts and the feedback of others about what might be causing that resistance.

2. Flatlining

This kind of structural problem occurs when a roller coaster works well for a while, but then the pillars begin missing the bell, and eventually the entire roller-coaster structure loses upward build or forward momentum.

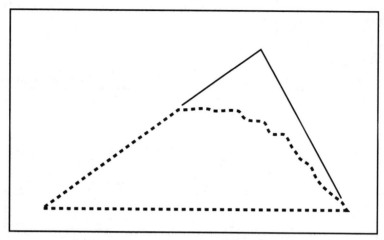

Figure 14-2 "Flatlining"

Ironically, the film *Flatliners* created exactly this kind of roller coaster for me. The first near-death experience was fascinating, and the second was also interesting. But after a while, the various experiences failed to be significantly different, and eventually I lost interest in their overall impact because there wasn't enough new information. As with most structurally flatlining stories, they don't really flatline, they actually decline because of the cumulative audience disappointment.

Flatlining is usually caused by problems with new information, especially in the areas of exciting plot complications or richer character reactions. Make sure that you're giving the hero new obstacles and challenges, not just more of the same.

3. Swiss Cheese

This kind of structural problem occurs when the roller-coaster ride works well for a while, then suddenly becomes very wobbly, then stabilizes again. These interruptions can be repeated several times within the story.

As an example, a light love scene just before the climax of the same scene could destroy the overall emotional build because the dramatic stakes aren't high enough.

This kind of structural problem tends to be a problem with conflict resolution because the audience feels that either the plot logic or the character's emotional arc isn't tracking. It can also be caused by problems with subplots and secondary characters who either overwhelm the main story or are not well integrated or justified.

4. Dive-Bomb

This roller coaster builds well almost to the climax, then becomes contrived and implausible, and the credibility of the entire story collapses.

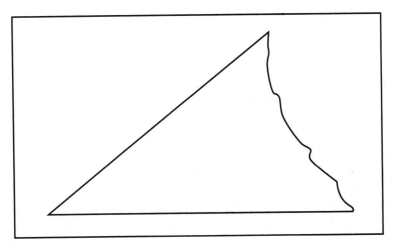

Figure 14-3   "Dive-Bomb"

This tends to be a problem with completion. The sinking sensation is caused by an unconvincing ending, so examine whether the actual pivotal moment, climax, and end result seem too contrived, whether it's failing to resolve all the problems your story has presented, or if the problem is simply that the audience hasn't been given enough setups to make the final payoffs work.

■ Decide Where to Fix ■

It's usually not too hard to tell where the problems are. But where you notice a problem and where the problem is caused aren't always the same thing.

For example, let's say you've given your script to three different readers, and they all feel that there is a scene, just before the climax, where the hero's actions are implausible or unjustified. Your roller coaster has a Swiss cheese problem; and if you were going to graph that roller coaster, it would look something like this:

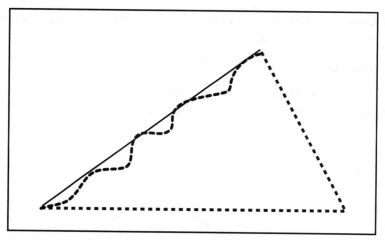

Figure 14-4 "Swiss Cheese Roller Coaster"

As a result, many writers would automatically begin to rewrite the scene where the sag is evident. However, the reason the scene is not working may have nothing to do with the way that it is written. Because of the cumulative impact of story information, the problem may occur much earlier in the story. Usually the power of the moment comes from what the audience already knows or cares about in the script, so you need to back up and learn why they don't like the character. Try to get at the cause of the dissatisfaction.

First identify the location of the problem, and then ask "Why?" That is the clue as to what element is not working. Once this is identified, you can go back and ask "What if the character did this or said that?" Always try to fix the problem as early in the story as possible, before the audience's cumulative frustration or confusion has a chance to build.

■ Decide How to Fix ■

When a roller coaster isn't working, it's because the pillars aren't as high as the author expected them to be, so there are four things that you can do with your story pillars to make that section of roller coaster maintain the right height. You can *add, subtract, switch the order,* or *rebuild pillars* in a way to strengthen the emotional experience for the audience.

Here are examples of the four basic options you can consider as you try to strengthen your roller coaster:

1. Adding

One way to strengthen your roller coaster is by adding a story pillar that contains information needed for a later scene to work.

For example, let's say that several people tell you that a major fight scene between a couple isn't working for them. The reason might be that you have failed to make it clear that the husband has a long history of being overly possessive. Once the audience understands the magnitude of that issue within the marriage, then the later scene will work well.

2. Subtracting

Another way to fix a roller coaster is to subtract information from the audience's awareness. For example, if the audience is failing to be surprised by the big discovery of a syringe in the suspected murderer's closet, then a possible solution is to eliminate the scene much earlier in the story in which the audience is told that the suspect is a diabetic.

Another reason to eliminate something from your script is if it snags your attention in a way that distracts from the story. Somerset Maugham was quoted as saying, "Cut if at all possible." If it bothers you, trust your instincts. Anything that can be cut should be cut in order to keep momentum going.

3. Switching Order

The point of switching pillars is that sometimes the same story information, given in a different order, can have greater impact for the audience. Often the order is more a matter of preference. One television producer I've worked with preferred to surprise the audience with the arrival of the police during a crime scene, while his partner preferred to cut away to the cops at intervals to heighten the tension of whether the cops and crooks would meet up. Neither way is "right"; each creates very different sensations in the audience and demands an entirely different storytelling technique. Be aware of the subtleties of sequence; consider alternatives and ask yourself which way would work better for your script. Pay close attention to this dynamic, especially if there is a segment where the feedback you've had suggests that the roller coaster dips around that point. Changing the order of events may just solve the problem.

4. Rebuilding

Sometimes the information you've decided to tell the audience is the right information but your readers didn't understand what was happening because of the way the scene is written. Another possibility is that the moment is more ambiguous than you intended. Or perhaps even your readers are misunderstanding what you meant to imply. In such cases, just rewrite the same scene in a less confusing way.

This is an important point because sometimes writers think the comment "I don't understand" means "I don't agree with the character's motivation or the plot's logistics." However, it often just means "I don't understand the meaning of that line," or "I am not comprehending the logistics of this sequence."

Q U E S T I O N S

1. What feedback have you gotten on your roller coaster?

2. Does your roller coaster capture your dramatic center?

3. Does your roller coaster convey your dramatic equation?

4. Which category would most of your notes fall into?
   New information?
   Bonding?
   Conflict resolution?
   Completion?
   Where in the script are most problems located?

5. If you were going to graph it, how would it look?
   Slow start?
   Flatlining?
   Swiss cheese?
   Dive-bomb?

6. Which techniques would strengthen your roller coaster?
   Adding pillars?
   Subtracting?
   Switching?
   Rebuilding?

Final Words

I had a theater professor who used to say, "Don't go into theater unless there's nothing else you can stand to do!" It drove me crazy at the time, but now I know why he was so insistent. Show business is a rough business, and there are few occupations with more potential for hard work and disappointment. Even being at the top is a bumpy ride, and struggling to get there can be very tough indeed.

So don't write because you think screenwriting is a quick and easy way to fame and fortune. Don't do it for the money, or the glamour, or the power, or for any reason—unless you have a passion for the work. Do it for the story. For the product. For the process. For the truths in you that must be told.

Every society has had its storytellers. It is an ancient and honorable role, one that provides a crucial service to society. Our century's "story hearth" has been film and television, but the emotional needs storytellers fulfill have been the same throughout history.

What humans need is catharsis. They need the emotional release, the venting of frustrations, and the overwhelming yet pleasurable sense of being completely drained after their internal tension has built to a peak, then subsided. Deep in the human genetic memory people recognize the patterns that reflect the rhythms of life and death, in which sensations move to a peak and then fade away. Experiences such as sex, joy, grief, and even pain are all patterns of tension and release as primal and fundamental as existence itself.

Humans are so hungry for cathartic patterns that they long for them at the deepest levels, beyond words, logic, conscious understanding, or rational analysis. Daily life once provided countless opportunities to experience such intense emotions. The struggle for food, the awareness of possible danger, or tribal rituals offering meaning and release kept primitive humans in touch with a wide range of appropriate and socially acceptable emotions. Until recently, most families still dealt with life's traumas at home. Births, deaths, joyful honeymoons, or terrifying illnesses usually were part of everyday life, so people had frequent opportunities to experience both the wonders and terrors of existence at close range.

Modern society has distanced most of us from these natural occurrences, so emotions now build up with few legitimate or socially approved avenues of release. Yet our primal needs remain. If people don't find appropriate outlets, they will create some other way to vent those feelings—through violence, chemical addiction, or resignation.

People also need hope. They need inspiration. They long for role models of courage and greatness, happiness and wholeness, meaning and faith. In fact, for humans stories are the opportunity to find meaning in their lives. People don't make time to read Nietzsche or Hume, Einstein or Freud. What they do make time for are stories. Films. TV. Soap operas. Sitcoms. Movies of the Week. In the continuous effort to "make life make sense," people reach for stories. To obtain clarity, affirmation, enjoyment, and release.

Look at the impact the entertainment industry has had. Archie Bunker's chair is in the Smithsonian. *M.A.S.H.* helped the peace movement coalesce. Fashion was dominated by the torn sweatshirts of *Flashdance* and the goofy sweetness of *Annie Hall. JFK* got sealed government files opened, and *The Burning Bed* brought wife abuse to a new height of national consciousness. The specifics of the challenge each human faces may differ, but the underlying fundamentals of life, birth, death, loss, and success will never change. What changes is how the audience learns to see and value them. As one of society's storytellers, you must learn how to express what they mean to you.

So be bold. Be daring. Don't follow formulas. Don't build the same roller coaster again and again. The one thing you have to offer is your voice, your perceptions. The entertainment business needs stories, films, and television shows that move, delight, and create adventures for viewers' minds, emotions, and souls. That kind of "soul contact" is not possible without the passion, imagination, and originality that each writer has to contribute.

That's why Hollywood needs you. This book is dedicated to the goal of helping you gain access to your highest level of creativity and craft, because the world needs to hear what you need to say.